CAVALRY

V. VUKSIC ◇ Z. GRBASIC

CAVALRY

THE HISTORY OF A FIGHTING ELITE

650BC – AD1914

CASSELL

A CASSELL BOOK

First published in the UK
1993 by Cassell
Villiers House
41/47 Strand
London
WC2N 5JE

Distributed in the United States
by Sterling Publishing Co., Inc.
387 Park Avenue South, New York, NY 10016–8810

Distributed in Australia
by Capricorn Link (Australia) Pty Ltd
P.O. Box 665, Lane Cove, NSW 2066

British Library Cataloguing-in-Publication Data
A catalogue record for this book is available from
the British Library

ISBN 0-304-34041-3

TRANSLATED BY SRDJAN VUJICA

Half-title: Hungarian cavalryman in national costume, nineteenth century
Frontispiece: Knight in tournament armour, beginning of sixteenth century

Typeset by RGM Typesetting, Southport

Printed and bound in Hong Kong

CONTENTS

LIST OF COLOUR PLATES

INTRODUCTION

Horses have been serving man for over 5,000 years – ever since the late Neolithic period. They have carried into battle warriors, conquerors, kings and the great military commanders, and countless empires and states were created and destroyed with their help. There is an indissoluble connection between the history of civilization and the service of horses to man.

Cave drawings and paintings support the theory that horses became domesticated in the fifth millennium BC, in Central Asia (now various republics of the old Soviet Union). They were probably first tamed by the Aryans, a nomadic people of Indo-European origin and, in the third millennium BC, with the migration of the Indo-Europeans, the horse arrived in Asia Minor and Europe.

In the beginning, this domesticated horse, close in size to the pony, served the nomads by providing meat, milk and leather; even today, peoples in these areas of Asia breed New Kirgiz, Kushumsky, Bashir and other stock for these purposes. Later on, probably for practical reasons, a horseherd (so to say) climbed on the back of one of his animals: he could look after more animals at once, take them to farther grazing-grounds or flee with his herd when danger threatened. The nomads gradually realized that horses were valuable not only as livestock but for their speed. The earliest written record of domesticated horses, which implies that they were also used for riding, comes from China, in the third millennium BC, and concerns nomads living in what is now Mongolia.

At the beginning of the second millennium BC, at the dawn of the biblical era, one of the Aryan tribes – the Mitanni – founded a state in Asia Minor between the upper reaches of the Tigris and Euphrates rivers. They brought with them horses from their ancestral regions, and raised them in warm and fertile surroundings. The Mitanni were known for racing horses and chariots drawn by teams of two, which indicates a high level of horsemanship.

North of the Mitanni, in part of present-day Turkey, lived the warrior tribe of the Hittites. They had discovered the technology of bronze processing and were far ahead of their neighbours in the manufacture of weapons. The Hittites were not interested in the horse *per se*, but realized that a horse-drawn chariot, carrying a crew of soldiers, had great military potential. At first they bought horses from the Mitanni; later, they were able to breed them for themselves. They built sturdy, single-axis chariots which carried three crew members: the driver and two warriors. The combat chariots were organized into special units by the Hittites, and became their elite corps, capable of undertaking independent action at great distances.

Their expansion soon brought them into conflict with the Semitic tribes of the Amorites, Arabs and Canaanites, who lived on the Mediterranean shore, on the territory of Palestine and part of Syria. The performance of the chariots in battle was so convincing that the Semitic tribes adopted them very quickly. Around 1650BC, a group of Semitic tribes, known collectively as the Hyksos, conquered Egypt. They were equipped with high-quality bronze weapons – and chariots. The Hyksos moved 'faster than the news' down the Nile valley and captured the unprepared Egyptian towns one by one. It took Egypt 250 years to free itself from these conquerors; one of their legacies was the use of horses and chariots for combat.

South of the Mitanni state, in what is now Iraq, in Mesopotamia, between the middle and lower reaches of the Tigris and Euphrates, the Babylonian Empire flourished. It was ruled by the Amorites, one of the Semitic warrior tribes, the inheritors of the rich and ancient culture of the Sumerians, who had not known of horses.

In 1530BC, the Kassites, related to the Mitanni, came out of the mountains north-east of the Tigris, conquered Babylon and destroyed the Amorite state. The Kassites used horses for transport and to draw chariots, and they also had horseback units. We do not know what their riders looked like, or whether they used their horses for combat as well.

At about the same time, a people related to the Kassites conquered the ancient state in the Ind valley. Within a relatively short timespan, independently of one another, three of the oldest civilizations of ancient times had succumbed to the wave of change.

The horse undoubtedly played a part in the exit of these states from the world stage, but none of these civilizations was destroyed; the conquerors were quickly assimilated or departed after making their own contributions to civilized development.

In 1365BC, the Hittites conquered the Mitanni state, and a period of power equilibrium and local wars ensued, during which there were no important territorial changes.

Towards the middle of the fourteenth century BC, three states were contiguous in the biblical region: Egypt, which had conquered part of Palestine; the Hittite kingdom, which had annexed Syria and part of the upper reaches of the Tigris and Euphrates, and the Babylonian Empire under the Kassites. All had well-organized standing armies of infantry, chariots and several hundred horsemen. Ancient sources mention many battles, but exaggerate wildly the number of soldiers taking part. Hundreds of thousands of infantry are mentioned, and tens of thousands of combat chariots, but horsemen are mentioned only in numbers ranging from a few hundred to one or two thousand. Cavalry, it seems, were not yet an important military component.

CAVALRY
History, Tactics and Organization

By 1000BC men mounted on horses were an integral part of the armies of established and aspiring powers, but for about fifteen hundred years the cavalry was regarded as an adjunct to the infantry. Although sometimes treated as an independent force – by Philip II of Macedonia and Hannibal Barca, for example – no general rules were formulated for its organization and role in battle.

The ascendancy of the cavalry is thought by some historians to date from the Battle of Adrianople (378) when the Visigoths defeated the Romans; not until the fourteenth century was there a renaissance of the infantry.

Views on the use of cavalry did not change significantly after 1815, despite the increasing powers and accuracy of firearms, nor indeed had the weapons used changed much by the mid-nineteenth century: spears were still in use in some major European regiments, including the British lancers.

Army commanders stubbornly continued to believe that combat on horseback was primary, even at the beginning of World War I. Among the realities of machine-guns, barbed wire and trenches, cavalrymen 'dismounted, abandoned their horses, and continued the war on foot'.

DOMINANCE OF THE INFANTRY, 1000BC–AD450

ASSYRIANS

After the fall of the Mitanni kingdom in the middle of the fourteenth century BC, the Assyrian state, located in what is now northern Iraq, beyond the upper reaches of the Tigris, shed the chains of its vassalage. In the period of the early Empire, up to 883BC, Assyria went through several cycles of rise and fall. It conquered Mesopotamia and Syria, defeated the Hittites and took Babylon, and then lost them all.

Kings Assurnasirapli II (883–59), Shalmaneser III (858–24) and Sargon II (722–05) were mainly responsible for the organization of the New Assyrian Empire and its military power.

During their reigns, Assyria was a typical warrior state, more powerful than any other of the period in Asia Minor. Its military might rested on its hardy steppe population; since the dawn of time, dexterity with the bow and arrow had been a condition of their survival. The steppes were the recruiting ground for the core of the Assyrian army – the infantry, armed mainly with long-range weapons but capable of fighting from chariots or on horseback. At first, the Assyrian army consisted of a militia called up only

Median cavalryman, third century BC

Scythian horse archer, fourth century BC

in the event of war, but from the ninth century on a standing royal army was formed.

In the beginning, they were solely infantrymen. King Tiglathpileser I (1112–1074) had at his disposal horse-drawn combat chariots, which he used for long-range operations. Assurnasirapli increased the mobility and penetration of his army by creating a cavalry force which replaced the chariots. Accounts of armies over 100,000 strong, with 1,000 chariots and 10,000 riders date from his rule. Several accounts point to the conclusion that about 10 per cent of the Assyrian field army was on horseback.

Insurrections of the enslaved peoples weakened Assyria, and it no longer had the strength to hold on to the areas it had conquered. In 612BC, an army of Medes and Scythians destroyed the capital of Nineveh, and Assyria ceased to exist.

PERSIANS

In the ninth century BC, the huge plateau between the Caspian Sea and the Persian Gulf was inhabited by nomadic Iranian tribes. They blended with the original inhabitants, and named the plateau Iran. There were several tribes: Medes, Persians, Bactrians, Parthians, Scythians, Sogdinians and Sacaes.

The Medes, who inhabited western Iran, founded the first Iranian state towards the end of the seventh century BC. The Greek historian Herodotus considers King Cyaxares (625–585) the founder of the state and the creator of the Median army, which, following the Assyrian example, he divided into separate infantry and cavalry units. His heir could not withstand the onslaught of King Cyrus II (559–29) who united Persia, conquered Media, vanquished Lydian King Croesus and finally took Babylon in 539. Cyrus's son Cambyses continued his father's conquests, and conquered Egypt in 525.

After consolidating Persian gains, King Darius I (521–486) reorganized the state and army. His kingdom consisted of conquered peoples, whom Darius allowed to keep their systems and customs. He divided the country into twenty provinces under the rule of governors called satraps, and in the event of war each province raised its own army, which was placed under the king's command. Besides these provincial forces, the king also had a standing mercenary army of 10,000 infantry called Immortals (because their numbers were kept constant at this level) and in addition 2,000 infantry and 2,000 horsemen of the guard.

The Persian heavy cavalry was made up of riders from Bactria, Media, Armenia and Persia – about 15,000 strong, and usually occupied a space in the centre of the Persian battle formation. The light cavalry consisted of nomadic horsemen inhabiting the Iranian plateau – Parthians, Arachosians, Dahaes, Sacaes, Bactrians, and the Scythians, who lived beside the Black Sea. These detachments usually numbered about 2,000 men, except for the Scythians, whose numbers sometimes reached 5,000. As the armament of the light cavalry was intended for long-distance combat with bow and arrow and, more rarely, javelins, and because their protective equipment was poor – mostly woven shields, and only occasionally scale armour – they fought in loose order. They were placed on the flanks of the battle formation, but were not entrusted with operational tasks. Pillaging tended to distract them from the battle and the exploitation of initial successes.

GRAECO-MACEDONIANS

At the time when waves of nomadic and warrior tribes arrived in Asia Minor from the Euro-Asian steppes, the area of the Aegean Sea was colonized by the Greeks. They blended with the indigenous population, and replaced their so-called Myceneaen culture of building royal palaces and temples with their own Hellenic culture, which stressed the erection of cities (*polis*), which then became independent city-states. Kings were replaced by public functionaries who represented the people (*demos*). This, however, did not prevent the feeling among Greeks of belonging to people of the same origin, and this was reflected in their common name – the Hellenes.

Although operating in a closed arena, without external influences, Greek weaponry and military skills were honed in constant internecine conflicts. The first serious opponent to confront the Greeks from outside their world was the Persian Empire.

Up to the time of the Persian Wars (500–479BC), cavalry had developed only in Thessaly and Boeotia, where conditions for breeding horses were more favourable. Just before the Peloponnesian War (431–04), there were 1,200 horsemen in Athens, and the ranks of the cavalry were filled from the middle classes: men who could afford to buy and keep their own horses. The basic tactical unit was the *phyla*, commanded by a *phylarchos*, and the whole cavalry was two *hipparchoi*, each with five *phyloi*.

In Sparta, cavalry formed at the time of the Peloponnesian War, numbered about 400 men, who formed for battle in a square. In Thessaly and Boeotia (Thebes) cavalry was divided into armoured and unarmoured, i.e. heavy and light, according to weaponry and protective equipment. The basic unit was the *ile*, consisting of 64 men, formed in 15 files and four ranks. The Thessalonians formed the ile either in the shape of a rhomb, suitable for flanking and attacking the rear, or as a column for penetrative attacks.

The Boeotian cavalry had a prominent role in the time of Epaminondas (418–362). At the Battle of Leuctra (371), he deployed it in support of the left flank of his formation, and with a column of heavy infantry, it broke through the Spartan phalanx and decided the outcome. At Mantinea (362), 1,500 Boeotians on the left flank and 1,500 Thessalonians on the right drove off the enemy cavalry and executed a flanking attack on the opposing infantry formation, thus contributing to the victory over Sparta and Athens.

From the middle of the fourth century BC, Macedonia was the leading power in Greece, and often interfered in the internal affairs of the disunited Greek states. Philip II of Macedonia (382–36) based his power on a standing national army, cavalry and infantry, ready for action at any moment. He reorganized the Macedonian cavalry, and turned it into a separate branch of the army equal to the infantry.

The heavy cavalry, whose role was to strike, was made up of noblemen (Companions or *heteroi*) with lances and swords and protected by breastplates. Recruitment was territorial, and each county was supposed to give one ile, which in wartime had 200 horsemen. Philip recruited his light cavalry from annexed Thracian provinces; these were armed with a lance 3–4 m/10–13 ft long (*sarissa*), and their role was reconnaissance, hence their name, scouts (*prodromoi*). At the Battle of Chaeronea (338), the Theban

Thracian light cavalryman, fourth century BC

phalanx was broken by a strike of 1,800 men of the Macedonian heavy cavalry commanded by Alexander the Great (337–23), Philip's son.

Although the Greek states had more people, a stronger economy and greater military experience, they could not find adequate political and military organization to resist the mounting pressure from Macedonia. After the Battle of Chaeronea, where he defeated the Athenians and Thebans, Philip achieved supremacy over all Greece, which was united in the Pan-Hellenic alliance, based in Corinth. All the states save Sparta were members. It was Philip's desire to start a campaign against his traditional enemy, Persia. The Graeco-Macedonian alliance accepted this, and after Philip's death Alexander started for Asia at the head of 30,000 infantrymen and 5,000 cavalry. The heavy cavalry consisted of the Companions (1,800), Thessalonian noblemen (1,700), and Greeks (600); the light cavalry was made up of 1,000 Thracian prodromoi.

Greek cavalry operated in close coordination with the infantry phalanxes, while the Macedonian was independent, under the direct command of Alexander, and used for special tasks, which included attacking the opposing cavalry and infantry. Sometimes its role was decisive, as at Granicus (334) and Gaugamela (331). Alexander also used his cavalry for pursuit, and after the Battle of Gaugamela, it covered 75 km/47 miles in a single day. By pursuing Darius III through Media and Bactria the cavalry prevented the enemy's reorganization.

CARTHAGINIANS

Carthage was an ancient town and state on the Mediterranean shores of Africa, now Tunisia. It was founded in 814BC as a colony of the Phoenician city of Tyre, and developed thanks to its superb geographic position, well protected from land and sea, and to the rich soil in its hinterland, with abundance of potable water. From the seventh century BC, Carthage became the most powerful state in the Mediterranean basin, its military might based on mercenaries from Numidia, Tunisia, Algeria, Libya, Morocco and Mauritania. As both Carthaginians and Greeks colonized islands and coastal areas in the Mediterranean, clashes were inevitable.

In the third century, the Roman Empire was sufficiently strong to oust the Greeks from the stage, and to take on Carthage. The expansionist policies of both countries led to the Punic Wars, the most important of which was the Second (218–01).

After naval defeat by the Romans, Carthage raised a strong army, organized by one of the greatest military commanders of his time, Hannibal Barca (247–183). Knowing that his force would be up against the superior Roman infantry, he devoted great attention to the cavalry, which he turned into an equal and independent branch of the army. In numbers, it reached one-quarter of the infantry's strength, and was divided into heavy and light cavalry. The Carthaginian heavy cavalry's striking power recalled the cavalry of Macedonia, but with more mobility, while the Numidian light cavalry was extremely mobile. When Hannibal arrived on the Apennine peninsula, he had under his command 5,000 Celtic and 2,000 Spanish heavy cavalry, and 4,000 Numidian horsemen. Their commanders were experienced professionals, Hannon and Hasdrubal.

In the battles of the Second Punic War, the Carthaginian cavalry was the decisive element, not even balking at independent attacks on the enemy

Iberian (Spanish) cavalryman, third century BC

infantry. At the Battle of Cannae (216), as part of a daring overall tactical plan, it broke the Roman cavalry and struck at the phalanxes from the rear, thus tipping the scales. Even in later periods of the war, when it was outnumbered, it successfully decoyed the Roman cavalry from the battlefield at the Battle of Zama (202).

ROMAN EMPIRE

The origins of the Roman Empire in the eighth century BC are shrouded in legend. The oldest state comprised the city of Rome and its environs, and in 510, the last of the seven kings was overthrown and Rome became a republic ruled by two consuls; in war they were supreme military commanders.

During the period of the republic, the Roman cavalry was among the weakest of its time. Rome had 84 centuries of infantry, and only 6 centuries of cavalry. The largest independent military formation – the legion – had 4,200 infantry and only 300 cavalry. The basic cavalry units were *turmae*, with 30 riders, armed with spears, and protected with helmets, leather armour and shields. Cavalry usually formed on the edges of the phalanx, most often in five ranks of 30 men each side, and protected its flanks. It was not rare for them to dismount and fight on foot.

In the third century BC, a special caste of knights (*equites*) was formed. These were rich men, who served in the cavalry; their commander was called the master of horse (*magister equites*).

After the Punic Wars, the Roman cavalry was replaced by that of their allies (*socii*), the Gauls, Celts and Germans.

After the end of the Civil Wars, Octavian Augustus (27BC–AD14) became undisputed ruler of Rome, and the republic became an empire. During his reign, the Roman Empire spread over Europe, Asia and Africa, taking in all the Mediterranean countries, most of those on the Black Sea, and southern and central Europe up to the Rhine–Danube line. To protect the borders of this huge empire, Octavian stationed all 25 legions in fortified border garrisons. Apart from these principal troops, Rome had auxiliary forces (*auxilia*), archers and horsemen. The role of the horsemen was to patrol and secure the borders, and they were organized in special units called *alae* (wings), commanded by a *praefectus*. The basic units were still the turmae; larger units were the *quinquenaria* (500 men), consisting of 16 turmae, and *miliaria* (1,000), with 24 turmae. Riders serving in the mixed infantry/cavalry units (*cohortes equitatae*) were not as well equipped or mounted. They numbered 400 infantry and 128 cavalry.

Towards the end of the third century AD, the borders of the Roman Empire were swamped by various peoples – Goths, Alamanni, Franks, Vandals, Slavs, Quadi, Markomanii, Burgundians and others: jointly known as barbarians. Rome began taking the allied peoples of the border areas into its military service, and the infantry's fighting value declined. The consequence was an increase in the cavalry; Gallienus (260–68) created large units which became important in battle, especially in the second half of the fourth century. The frequent incursions of the barbarians could be countered only by replacing the static fortified defence with mobile units, such as cavalry. In 378, at the Battle of Adrianople, Emperor Valens fielded 30,000 infantry and 10,000 cavalry against the Goths.

The barbarian onslaught so weakened Rome that in 476 the Western Roman Empire fell.

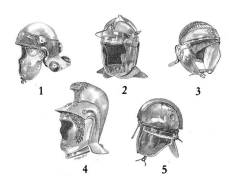

Roman cavalry helmets
1 *Iron helmet of auxiliary cavalry type B, second quarter of first century AD*
2 *Iron helmet of auxiliary cavalry type E, end of first to mid-second century AD*
3 *Iron helmet of auxiliary cavalry type A, first half of first century AD*
4 *Bronze helmet of cavalry sports type G, late second to early third century AD*
5 *Iron cavalry helmet of Romano-Sassanian type, late third to fourth century AD*

Roman heavy cavalryman, fourth century

CAVALRY ASCENDANCY AD450–1500

PARTHIANS AND SASSANIDS

The Parthians were a semi-nomadic people of Iranian origin who, in the first millennium BC, settled in the south of Hyrcania, south-east of the Caspian Sea, in what is now Iran. They were ruled by Assyria, India, Persia, Macedonia and the kingdoms of Alexander's successors (the Diadochi). They served in the Persian standing army, and in Alexander's army at the time of his Indian campaign.

Under the leadership of King Arsaces I, the Parthians rose in 247BC and formed an independent state around the city of Hercatompylos, which soon spread to the Caspian Sea and the banks of the Indus river. Wars with neighbouring states were frequent, and the borders of the kingdom widened. During the reign of Mithridates I (171–38), Parthia extended its rule over Bactria, Persia and Media, and Mithridates II (124–87) consolidated these conquests.

The country did not have a unified administrative system and was divided into 18 regions. Mithridates II reorganized the Parthian army, replacing mercenaries with men dependent on the king and his vassals. The main part of the army was the cavalry, again divided into heavy and light. The light horsemen were excellent riders and bowmen; characterized by great mobility and nomadic tactics in war, they avoided direct clashes with enemy cavalry, attacked suddenly in a hail of arrows, retreated as suddenly, and then returned from all sides. They rode without any protection, and carried a bow, a sword and a knife. The heavy cavalry consisted of the nobility (cataphracts), armed with long lances and protected by coats of chain mail and scales, and mounted on strong horses, probably Nisaean chargers, also mail or scale clad. Their tactics were different from those of the light cavalry – they charged the enemy head on.

From 54BC to AD218, the Roman Empire waged seven unsuccessful wars against the Parthian state, and one of the worst defeats in Roman history was at the hands of the Parthians, at Carrhae, in 53BC. A Parthian cavalry army, with 1,000 cataphracts and 8,000 horse archers, destroyed a Roman force of 4,000 cavalry and 28,000 infantry.

The wars with the Romans so exhausted the Parthian state that it was conquered by Sassanid Persia in AD227. The period of Sassanid rule was characterized by difficult wars against Rome, Byzantium, India, the Turks, Arabs and other nomadic tribes, as well as by internal conflicts among the rulers, the nobility and the priests. In this centralized state, the army was financed from the king's treasury, and the most important part was the cavalry inherited from the Parthians. Warriors were a special social caste, and the heavy cavalry were recruited from among the nobility, the light being made up of nomads from the Iranian plateau. It was organized in special units of several thousand men, and their tactics were very similar to those of the Parthians.

After defeat in the war with Byzantium, Sassanid Persia was conquered by Muslim Arabs in 637.

Parthian horse archer, second century

GOTHS

The Goths were the most powerful east Germanic tribe, who inhabited Scandinavia and the Baltic areas. In the first century AD they moved to the lower reaches of the Vistula river and from there to the north shores of the Black Sea in search of better living conditions. In the course of these migrations, they split into two groups: Ostrogoths, east of the Dniester river, and Visigoths, between the Dniester and the Danube. Together, they had a military force of between 10,000 and 15,000 men.

At the beginning of this period of southward migrations, the Goth cavalry was subordinate to the infantry. Its horsemen were poorly dressed, used wickerwork shields, and were armed with spears and only rarely bows. They rode bareback, and it was not rare for them to fight on foot; on these occasions, the well-trained horses waited for them, but sometimes the horsemen were followed by infantry holding the horses' manes.

Having settled in their new habitats, the Goths formed alliances with the native Sarmatians and Alans, and became serious enemies of the Roman Empire. Their first conflicts took place at the beginning of the third century. The Goths staged raids into Roman territory and plundered the provinces of Moesia and Dacia, going as far as Greece. They defeated the Roman general Decius, but were in turn defeated by Emperor Claudius II, at Naissus (269). However, they kept up constant pressure, and in 275 Aurelian had to cede to them Dacia (most of what is now Romania).

Goths were taken into the service of Rome just like other peoples living along the empire's borders, but under pressure from the new wave of nomadic invaders, the Huns, the Visigoths moved towards Moesia. Emperor Valens tried to stop them, but was defeated and killed at Adrianople in 378. The most prominent role in the Goth victory belonged to the cavalry, and some historians consider this battle the moment when cavalry domination began.

Under the leadership of Alaric, the Goths advanced on Rome, but were decisively defeated.

TURANIAN NOMADS

The Turanians were a group of nomadic peoples consisting of two main sub-groups: Finno-Ugrian and Turco-Mongol. Their ancestral homeland was Turan – the territories delimited by the Arctic Ocean to the north, the Caspian Sea to the south and Pacific Ocean in the east. Forest covered most of the northern part of this area, Eurasian steppes the central part, and there were deserts in the south.

All Turanians had more or less the same social and military structure. They merged and split easily, blended with other peoples and were absorbed. They made a living by breeding animals, specially horses, and by robbery. They were excellent riders and archers, always ready for flight or fight. Their main weapon was the bow, but they also employed spears and curved sabres for close combat, and were adept at using lassoes and snaring wild animals. Metal or leather scale was known to them. As they moved very fast, the enemy could not catch up and engage them in battle; they tended to avoid hand-to-hand combat. To deceive an enemy, they would often simulate flight, then turn and strike, inflicting decisive defeats. They were also good at laying ambushes.

Under pressure of other nomadic tribes from Asia, the Turanian people started moving west in the fourth century. The first group to have a separate identity were the Huns, followed by the Bulgars in the fifth century and the Avars towards the middle of the sixth. These new groups turned towards Europe, bent on conquest, and their appearance on the borders of the Roman Empire hastened its downfall. On the other hand, direct contact with Rome led to changes in their social and economic structure, and they abandoned the nomadic way of life and settled in the Roman provincies, engaging in agriculture.

After conquering the Alans and Ostrogoths, the Huns founded their own state, stretching from the Alps to the Urals. Under Attila (441–53), this state reached the pinnacle of its power, but broke apart after his death and the Huns were assimilated by other peoples.

Towards the end of the sixth century the Bulgars created a state in the area of the Sea of Azov, but this disintegrated in the middle of the seventh century, and some of the tribes formed a new state between the Danube and Mount Balkan, an area already inhabited by the Slavs. Eventually, the Bulgars converted to Christianity and were assimilated by the Slavs, accepting even their language.

Around 560 the Avars, reinforced by Huns and Bulgars, crossed the Carpathians and entered the Pannonian Valley. Their power spread from the Adriatic Sea to Bohemia, but in 626 they were defeated by Byzantium at Constantinople; this was the beginning of the end of Avar supremacy. Finally crushed by the Franks in 796, they soon vanished from the world stage.

BYZANTINE EMPIRE

The Byzantine Empire, with its capital at Constantinople (now Istanbul), was created in the division of the Roman Empire into the Eastern and Western Empires in 395. When the Western Empire fell in 476, Byzantium became independent, and survived until 1453, but the great migrations of the fifth century shook Byzantium; weakened, it lost much of its territory. Under Emperor Justinian (527–65), who favoured the liberation of all lost territories and the restoration of the Roman Empire, Byzantium became the largest power in the Mediterranean.

At the time of Justinian, cavalry consisted of the private armies of Hun, Goth and local leaders (*foederati*), various barbarian units under a joint commander, and the allied troops (*socii*). The foederati were heavy cavalry, the rest light, and the cataphracts of Asia Minor were specially prominent. The basic administrative and tactical unit was the *tagma*, with about 300 riders. It consisted of three *hektakontarchiai*, each with a hundred men, and this in turn consisted of 10 *dekarchiai*. Usually three tagmas made up a higher tactical unit (*moira*), and three moiras made a *merarhia*, 3,000 men strong. According to the *Strategicon*, an eleventh century military manual, the Byzantine army usually had 30 tagmas, or about 9,000 horsemen. Four guard cavalry units (*tagmata*), about 1,500 men, were stationed in Constantinople: Scholae, Excubiti, Arithmos and Ikantoi.

Like the infantry, the mounted forces were armed for close- and long-range combat, and could be used either for cavalry strikes or fighting at a distance – very important in conflicts with the eastern peoples. Their armament consisted of a bow, long sword and lance, and they were protected by armour, helmet and vambraces for the arms and greaves for the legs. Towards the end of the sixth century, the equipment of the light and heavy units differed significantly: the light had a bow with a range of about 200 paces, a short sword and weak armour, while the heavy units were well protected and their principal weapon was a striking lance.

In the seventh century, Byzantium reorganized its administration and military commands along provincial lines (*themata*), and by the tenth century there were 46 themes, under the rule of governors (*strategoi* – generals). The westernmost themes were in the south of what are now Italy and the Adriatic states, and the easternmost in present-day northern Iraq. Each theme was responsible for providing a number of soldiers, usually several thousand; for a time, the Anatolikon, Thrakesion and Chaldia themes raised more than 10,000 each.

At the time of Leo VI (886–912) the heavy cavalry was specially well equipped and protected. Its men were armed with a broad sword, dagger, small bow and heavy lance with pennant, and the horses of officers and men of the first rank were partially armoured. According to the emperor's instructions, of five front-rank men, three were armed with lances and two with bows and forty arrows each. The basic unit was a banner (*bandon*), which consisted of six winglets (*allaghion*) of 50 each. Each allaghion had five dekarchiai of 10 men. Several bandons formed moira, and three moiras a *turma*, for a total of 6–7,000 troops.

A large number of mercenaries served in the Byzantine army, and in the eleventh century there were as many mercenaries as other troops: Saljuqs, Cumans, Pechenegs, Uzes, Alans, Bulgars, Italians, Venetians, Normans, Germans, Russians, Serbs and Arabs.

Byzantine cavalry was usually placed on the wings of infantry formations, and its decisive role was striking the enemy's flanks. Infantry generally fought with bows and arrows, rarely engaging the enemy in direct contact, and was therefore not considered of much account. At the Battle of Daras (530), the Byzantine cavalry routed the Persian mounted forces, having tipped the balance by attacking the enemy's flank. At Trycammarum (533), the imperial cavalry did not even wait for the infantry before attacking and destroying the Vandal cavalry. In the defensive Battle of Taginae (552), the barbarians employed by Byzantium (Langobards, Heruls and Gepids) dismounted and held back the Goth cavalry; fresh forces from the reserve were then thrust into the fray, and the battle was won.

However, Byzantine mounted forces could not cope with eastern light cavalry, which used nomadic tactics, and although reinforced by the Norman heavy cavalry, they were defeated at Manzikert (1071) by the Saljuq Turks.

ARABIANS

Before the appearance of Islam on the Arabian Peninsula, cohesive factors were already in operation there: the people were of the same race, spoke the same language, and had the same customs. The prophet Muhammad (*c.*570–632) added another: Islam, the new religion. By force and persuasion, he united Arabia under Islam, and placed himself at its head as the prophet of Allah. The struggle for primacy in Arabia did not reveal any particular degree of military effectiveness, either operational or tactical. However, it is said that those fighting on Muhammad's side had the advantage in discipline, firmness and enthusiasm. The Kur'an, the religious law of the

Pecheneg cavalryman, eleventh century

Norman knight in Byzantine service, from tenth to eleventh century

Muslims, makes it a duty of the faithful to wage war on the faithless until they are defeated or forced to pay tribute. Practically, the Kur'an calls for general conscription, and threatens penalties for those who fail to respond.

In only ten years, from 633 to 642, and with only some thousands of men, a vast and rich expanse, consisting of Persia, Syria and Egypt, was conquered. Apart from political unity, which made the Arabian conquest coherent, and the warrior spirit they brought from the desert, a reason for this astounding success must have been the weakness of their opponents, Byzantium and Persia, who had exhausted each other in mutual struggle.

Operations over such huge areas could be carried out only with large bodies of cavalry, and light cavalry was the mainstay of Arab fighting power. The desert light riders were basically individual fighters, unused to any tactical formation, so to enhance their effectiveness Muhammad spread the word that Allah looked favourably on those who fought in firm ranks. That this divine order was heeded was confirmed by Byzantine Emperor Leo IV, who wrote that the Arabs were the most skilled barbarian horsemen, and that their formations, shaped as elongated rectangles, were virtually impregnable.

In the seventh century, cavalry was divided into men armed with long lances, those with javelins, with bows, and with complete protective equipment – armour and sword. The best armed and equipped were in the first rank, the quality decreasing to the fifth, which was the poorest. The first and fourth rank fought in close order, while the rest held a loose formation. Combination of both forms was the characteristic of Arab cavalry.

The expansion of their state into foreign territory, inhabited by other peoples with different religions and customs, posed administrative problems which the Arabs could not solve. They had started out to conquer and pillage, but were culturally too advanced to do only that. By 718, they had conquered all of North Africa, Spain and Afghanistan, and had attacked Constantinople several times. In 732, 1,500 km/1,000 miles from their starting point, the Arabians ran out of steam, and were defeated at Poitiers by the army of Charles Martel.

From the eighth century, Arabian heavy battle cavalry was mostly armoured, partly in imitation of Persian and Byzantine forces, but mail coif, scale hauberk and lances were used with growing frequency. These forces could fight equally well on horseback and on foot. Light cavalry, mostly horse archers, was used for reconnaissance and raids. In time, their battle formation gained complexity, including infantry units and camel-mounted forces, but cavalry remained their main arm.

FEUDAL CAVALRY

After the fall of the Western Roman Empire in 476, parts of its territory were settled by Germanic tribes. In their new environment, with different economic patterns, they developed new social relationships. The military nobility (vassals) were awarded land by their ruler (senior) according to merit, in return for an obligation to outfit themselves and a certain number of soldiers, and to answer the ruler's call in the event of war. In the beginning, land was granted only for life-long use, but as early as the ninth century these estates became permanently owned (feuds) by some families. A feud could be inherited only by the eldest son and could not be shared among brothers.

Arab (Andalusian) heavy cavalryman, eleventh century

Horsemen, belonging to the richer classes and therefore better equipped, were more effective in combat, and became the mainstay of military power. Germanic tribes from the steppes of eastern Europe were particularly successful horsemen (Goths, Langobards, Gepids, Heruls), while those from the west were mainly infantry. Among the Visigoths, living between Gibraltar and the Loire, only the nobility and their retainers (*bucelarii*) were mounted. For protection, they used mail or scale armour, a helmet and a round shield. The Langobards, who inhabited Tuscany and the valley of the Po, were armed with a long spear (*kontos*) and broad sword (*spathion*). Apparently they also used maces, bows and javelins, and for protection helmets, mail coifs, and even gauntlets, not used by others for some considerable time. Sometimes, they dismounted to fight on foot, and then adopted a hedgehog formation. In 705, in conflict with Slavs, their nobility was destroyed because they did not dismount, even though the ground was unsuited to mounted fighting. The Franks inhabiting the left bank of the Rhine fought exclusively on foot until the sixth century; only dukes and their retainers were on horseback. In the Carolingian era (eighth to tenth century), however, mounted troops were the backbone of the military, while infantry had only a supporting role. Lances and swords were the principal weapons; bows were secondary. Light armour (*brunia*) was used for protection, along with a visorless helmet and shield. Armies did not number more than 5,000 or 6,000 cavalry, because its equipment was prohibitively expensive (a cavalryman's outfit, with horse, cost the equivalent of 40 cows). Also, at that time large armies could not operate over great distances; there were no tactical units; soldiers banded around their officers.

In western Europe, feudal organization gave rise to distinctions between the higher nobility (large landowners – counts, dukes, barons) and the lower nobility – knights or milites. Knights, better off than ordinary warriors, could afford heavy weaponry, equipment and horses, and pay the necessary servants, so they were more effective in combat. There were also closed organizations of knights' religious orders. From the twelfth century, the feudal system weakened, and knights often entered the service of wealthy barons.

Until then, the armament of knights consisted of a long double-edged sword and a short lance, which could double as a missile if needed. A throwing battle-axe was in general use, though in Britain, France and some northern parts of Europe the two-handed Norman heavy axe was used. From the end of the twelfth century, lances became longer (5 m/16 ft), and were steel-tipped. The double-edged sword was unchanged, except for the hilt, which was lengthened to make possible a two-handed hold. Daggers, which could slip between armour scales, became more popular, as well as short-handled maces with spiked iron balls. The axe remained in use and the battle hammer was introduced. While the knight's mounted retainers had a bow, javelin and, depending on resources, sword and lance, infantry were usually armed with bow or crossbow, and for hand-to-hand combat a lance, with or without shield, halberd and sword.

From the time of the Carolingians, protective equipment was developed steadily, and by the fifteenth century consisted of rigid plate armour with the necessary joints. Horses were armoured too: only the nose, ears and legs beneath the knees were free. On marches, the riders' and horses' heavy

Teutonic knight, beginning of fifteenth century

Norman knight, twelfth century

English mounted archer, end of fifteenth century

equipment was transported in wagons or on beasts of burden. Every knight had two or three horses; a light one he rode during marches, and a heavier steed mounted before the battle.

Although knights were individual fighters, and rather unsuited for group action, they adopted some specific tactical forms for greater effectiveness. There were three basic formations – wedge (*cuneus*), line (*en haye*) and swarm (*en fourragerus*). The **wedge** was a deep formation with 5 men in the first line, 7 in the second, 9 in the third, and so on. It was suitable for attacks because it could be reinforced from the rear; in those days, there were no reserves. The drawback was that only a limited number of knights (those in the first lines) could shine, and it was precisely glory that drew them to combat. They therefore preferred to fight in **line**, where everybody could take part simultaneously. The **swarm** – a loose formation – was the favourite, however, as it allowed individuals most space to distinguish themselves. The knight's tactics were simple: do or die; he could not leave a battlefield until only a single banner was flying. As his mobility was restricted, he had to be assisted by less encumbered soldiers, making up a supporting unit known as the *lance*.

Between the tenth and fourteenth centuries, the knights were unstoppable. Light cavalry and infantry could not stand up to them in frontal combat, and archers and crossbowmen could launch only a few arrows before being forced to flee, lest they be trampled under the chargers' hooves. In the last clash between the early feudal Anglo-Saxon infantry and the new feudal Norman cavalry, at Hastings in 1066, the cavalry defeated the infantry mainly with close-combat weapons.

There were no tactical units in feudal cavalry, so the most important thing was to get them all to the battlefield at the same time and keep them there until the end. Battles were decided by numbers and quality of men, not by manoeuvring. The knights often demonstrated their selfishness and desire to distinguish themselves by attacking too early or by staying on the field when the battle was already lost, as at Nicopolis in 1396. In the Hundred Years' War (1339–1453), the English achieved full cooperation between the cavalry, dismounted to fight on foot, and the infantry, armed with powerful bows, which laid the ground for their charges and held back the enemy during retreat. The most notable successes achieved with these tactics were against the French at Crecy (1346) and Agincourt (1415). The French tried to use these English tactics at Poitiers in 1356, but failed, as their dismounted riders were slow and clumsy in the attack.

The fourteenth century witnessed the renaissance of the infantry, which again appeared on the battlefield in firm formations. Armoured cavalry began to lose importance, and knights were defeated by excellent Swiss infantry. In 1315, at the Battle of Mogarten, infantrymen used their halberds to topple knights from their horses; it was then easy to kill the immobile fallen riders. At the beginning of the fifteenth century, the Germans could attack the Hussite wagon camps only on foot. The Hussites sheltered behind the wagons and greeted the attackers with a hail of stones and arrows, and then engaged in hand-to-hand combat with spears, halberds, axes, flails and maces. The Germans never succeeded against these tactics.

Western Slavs adopted cavalry in the ninth century. At that time, Moravians and Czechs had tribal armies, consisting mainly of the troops of chieftains (*zupan*); they were mounted but could not compare, in size, weaponry or equipment, with the German cavalry, and in numbers and tactics not even with the Bulgarian or Ugrian riders. Towards the end of the tenth century, Czech cavalry became feudal, earlier than in other Slav lands, but was still weak and ineffective. In Poland, however, it represented the main part of the army from the beginning of that century, and was made up of noblemen who were obliged to provide for and outfit a certain number of horsemen, according to their wealth. In the fourteenth century, after union with Lithuania and the annexation of the Ukraine, Poland introduced heavy and light cavalry, the heavy consisting of armoured noblemen, and the light of Cossacks and Tartars. In battle, the armoured men, like the western knights, formed the first line; the rest were behind.

Russian cavalry first appeared in 971, in a war against Byzantium, but it could not compare with the Byzantine armoured riders. In the eleventh century, it was organized according to the decimal system, and armed with short lance, sword, bow and large shield. Three centuries later, under Mongol influence, it became one of the main elements of the army, and at the Battle of Kulikovo (1380) against the Mongols, an attack by the Russian cavalry decided the outcome. From the end of the fourteenth century, it was more effective and its equipment improved. Armament consisted of a long lance with pennant, strong sword, battle-axe, bow and dagger; protection was provided by helmet, mail coif or hauberk and large kite shield. The Russian battle formation was akin to that of the Tartars: five groups of scouts (*polk*), centre, left wing, right wing, and rearguard (reserve).

Ugrian steppe riders came to Europe towards the end of the ninth century. Armed with bows and sabres, they laid the ground for their attacks with salvoes of arrows and finished with charges in closed order. Their cavalry slowly acquired the characteristics of the western knights. In the fifteenth century, during the reign of Matthias Corvinus, hussar light horsemen made their appearance.

Magyar (Hungarian) cavalryman, tenth century

MONGOLS

The origin and early history of the Mongols are legendary only, as is often the case with the peoples of central Asia; even the roots of the name are not clear. Modern history has generally accepted that it derives from the word *mong*, meaning brave, but the first authentic word on the Mongols comes from Chinese chronicles of the T'ang dynasty (618–907). Together with later records, they reveal that the Mongols, as a group of unconnected tribes (Naimans, Tartars, Merkits, Keraits), lived along the Herlan Gola river, now a border area between Mongolia and Manchuria in China.

In the twelfth century, the Mongol clan system broke down and large families (*aili*) separated from the clan groups, and became the basic units of social and economic structure. Grazing lands were still in joint ownership, but herds belonged to families. Private ownership led to stratification and the creation of aristocratic feudal families, and a gathering of heads of the wealthiest families (*nojons*) had absolute power in the tribe. They had their companies of armed retainers (*nukers*) whom they fed, clothed and armed, and who, in return, guarded them in war and hunting and ensured their power in the tribe. Ordinary families became increasingly dependent on the nojons, who began allotting pasture rights and offering protection from other tribes. For these services, they took regular tribute in cattle, goats and milk products. The strengthening of these relations led to the nojons

Polish knight, twelfth century

21

Mongol warrior, from twelfth to thirteenth century

becoming a specific type of cattle-raising/warrior feudal class. Defeated Mongol and non-Mongol tribes were obliged to pay tribute and render military service: tribal leaders of the vanquished became vassals of the victors. This led to the unification of large territories under the leadership of the militarily strongest tribe.

The decisive role in the unification of the Mongols was played by a group of north-eastern tribes, among whom the Taidjyut and their leader Temujin were particularly prominent. Temujin (whose name means 'the finest steel') used raw military power to bind the Mongol tribes under his leadership. The great assembly of chieftains (*Kurultai*) proclaimed him Genghis Khan, meaning very powerful khan, and by 1209 large parts of central Asia were under his rule.

The Mongols were excellent riders, very good shots both on horseback and on foot, hardy, temperate in their needs and adept at combat and war. Military organization was an important factor in their successful wars of conquest between 1211 and 1280. For military purposes, the whole Mongol territory was divided into three areas: the left wing in the east, Junghar; the right wing in the west, Barunghar; and the central area, Khol. These areas were organized according to the decade system, of which the largest unit (*tumen*) had 10,000 men. These were able to carry out independent sorties, and if needed for operational purposes, several tumens formed an army. Each had ten regiments of 1,000 men (*minghan*), each regiment ten companies of 100 (*jagun*), and each company ten squadrons of ten (*arban*). There was also a guard unit of 10,000 chosen men (*keshik*). Some tribes and clans were grouped into minghan or tumen units, which ensured the unity of the formations, and therefore of the whole Mongol army. On large expeditions, command was nominally awarded to members of the dynasty, but real control was exercised by experienced warriors like Yaba, Subotai and Mukuli.

Genghis Khan's army was exclusively equestrian. Later, infantry, artillery (catapults) and engineers were added. Some of the mounted units were intended for close combat, some only for combat at a distance, and their armament differed accordingly. Those destined for close combat were armed with a lance, provided with a hook for pulling opponents from their horses; a curved sabre with honed point, used both for cutting and thrusting; two bows, for shooting on foot and from horseback, with various types of arrows, depending on target and distance. They wore lamellar armour of cured leather. The units for long-range combat were usually armed only with bow and arrow, with a sabre sometimes added. They wore no armour, and used a shield only when on guard duty.

At the time of their great conquests, the Mongols had the best army in Asia. They undertook a series of aggressive wars, and the extent of the territories overrun places them among the greatest conquerors in history.

Between 1211 and 1234 they captured China and all of central Asia; by 1240, southern and central Russia had also fallen. In 1241, they set off towards Europe. At Szydlowec they defeated the united army of the Polish duchies, at Liegnitz that of the Polish and German knights and the Knights of the Teutonic Order, and at Sajo river the Hungarians. They devastated Moravia, Transylvania and Hungary, advancing as far as the Adriatic Sea. However, the death of Genghis Khan's successor, Ogodei (1229–41), stopped further conquests in Europe.

The Mongols pulled back to decide on a new leader. After a short period of peace, they destroyed the Caliphate of Baghdad in 1258, and captured a large part of Syria, but were defeated in 1260 at the Battle of Ain Jalut. This was the definitive end of their westward drive, but their expansion continued into southern China, which was taken in 1280. The Sung dynasty was overthrown, and Kublai Khan ascended the Chinese throne, founding the Yuan dynasty.

The Mongols prepared carefully for every military expedition, devoting special attention to gathering data about the political, economic and military situation in the country they intended to attack. Infiltration of agents into enemy ranks was common practice; their tasks included fomenting discontent and spreading insubordination. In war, they tended to avoid clashes with large and well organized enemy forces, often trying to outflank them and thrust deep into their rear, attacking their important centres. Thanks to their great manoeuvrability, they had easy advantage on the battlefield. Reconnaissance and security units were sent 50–100 km/30–60 miles in advance of the main force, and communications were maintained through mounted messengers.

No information exists on any organized battle fought by the Mongols, but it can be surmised that their tactics did not differ much from those of other nomadic peoples who had attacked Europe earlier. They were simply better organized and armed, and more adept at combining strikes and archery attacks. They executed their táctical operations flexibly and with precision.

Attacks were usually carried out in deep formation, most often in four lines. Prior to this, various demonstrations and manoeuvres were carried out to mislead the enemy. The attack usually began with salvoes of arrows, and continued with a charge, the aim of which was encirclement. Part of the armoured heavy cavalry, trained for close combat, was left in reserve, and used to deliver the decisive strike when the outcome was in the balance.

OTTOMAN EMPIRE

After the fall of the Saljuq state, destroyed by the Mongols in the middle of the thirteenth century, the Kayi tribe of Oghuz Turks, under the rule of Emir Osman I (1281–1326), founded a state on the territory of Anatolia. Defeating the Byzantine army at Koyunhisar in 1301, the Ottomans secured their state on the Sea of Marmara, with its capital at Brussa. During the rule of Emir Orkhan (1326–59), significant steps were taken to organize the state along military-feudal lines. The majority of the ruling class were small feudal lords (spahis), obliged to answer to the emir's (later the sultan's) call to war. Their class characteristics and military obligations were similar to those of European feudal lords; however, the hierarchical structure of their society was stronger, and their land holdings were not heriditary but had to be earned in battle. They were therefore personally interested in the further expansion of the state, and their response to the ruler's summons was more enthusiastic. Orkhan's reign also saw the formation of a mercenary guard, which at first had 2,400 men in four units. The light cavalry (akinji), was made up of volunteer shepherds who, before Orkhan, represented the only Ottoman military power; they were used for reconnaissance and pillaging raids. Later, the Delis, Tartars and Turcomans were added to the light cavalry.

Saljuq Ghulam cavalryman, twelfth century

Turkish riders handled their bows (*yayin*) very skilfully at full speed, and hurled javelins (*cirit*) with great force and precision. They were also armed with a spear (*mizark*), sabre (*kilic* or *simsir*), curved knife (*yatagan*) and light and heavy maces (*topuz* and *amud*). Light horsemen were armoured partially or not at all, while the rich spahis had armour for themselves and their horses. This was of Persian design, but Ottoman made, and consisted of steel plates of varying sizes connected by mail, forming an exceptionally flexible armour (*korazin*). Other types in use included scale (*pirahen ahenin*), lamellar (*cukal*), lamellar cuirass (*cevsen*), mail coif (*zirh*), mail hauberk (*zirk kulah*), vambraces (*kolluk*), round shields (*kalkan*), helmets (*cicak*) and a round metal plate for head protection which formed part of the mail hauberk.

In accordance with its dual role – offensive and defensive – Turkish cavalry took up positions in the second line. The palace regiments were in the centre, with the Asian spahis on the left and the European on the right. The vassal cavalry was beside them, and the wings were occupied by the light cavalry, parts of which were also detached in front as skirmish forces. In battles with the heavy European armoured cavalry, the brunt of the first attack was borne by the infantry; then the mounted units struck at the shaken opponent from the second line. The Ottomans defeated the Serbians at Kossovo (1389), the European Crusaders at Nicopolis (1396) and Varna (1444), and the Hungarians at Mohacs (1526). In this last battle, the numerically superior Ottomans put their weaker mounted units in the first line and the spahis in the second, and left the infantry in the third line.

In battle, the Turkish light cavalry acted like that of other nomadic peoples: they harassed the opponent with hit-and-run tactics, then made way for the strike of the heavy cavalry. Towards the middle of the sixteenth century, European armies began using firearms, and adopted tactics which stressed the cooperation of cavalry and infantry, together with planned artillery support. The Ottomans continued to face this approach with tactics and cavalry forces unchanged in four centuries. The erosion of their state was followed by battlefield failures, and defeats at Saint Gotthard (1664) and Vienna (1683) put paid to their offensive power.

MOUNTED FIREARMS, 1500–1650

Changes in the structure of feudal society, the strengthening of central authority, and the appearance of firearms all brought significant changes in the character and composition of armed forces. In the sixteenth century, armies were formed mainly from free mercenaries. Firearms became important, and the first artillery and engineering units appeared alongside the cavalry and infantry. Mercenary armies were more numerous than those of the knights.

The formation of feudal mercenary armies was aided by the development of trade and accumulated money. As early as the beginning of the twelfth century, English King Henry I concluded a contract with Robert le Frison, who undertook to perform military service beyond his feudal obligations for the king in exchange for money. The conversion of feudal armies into mercenary forces was even quicker in European absolutist states, where there was no obligation of personal answer to the king's call for war, particularly outside the country's borders. However, the feudal and mercenary systems coexisted for quite some time. In the thirteenth and fourteenth centuries, whole companies were formed of mercenaries, and besides feudal lords, there were adventurers and fallen noblemen. According to tactical needs, companies could include both cavalry and infantry, and cities or kings engaged the services of several companies, dismissing them when the fighting was over.

In France and Burgundy, *compagnies d'ordonnance* were created, each with about 600 mercenary cavalrymen. In tactics and organization, they were heavily influenced by the tradition of the knights. This type of cavalry could not fight against the reformed infantry, especially if it had been partially armed with firearms. Only heavy cavalrymen on armoured horses could attack successfully the firm ranks of the Swiss mercenary infantry. Light cavalry could be used in more profitable ways: attacking infantry and artillery on the march, or independently on the battlefield in favourable circumstances.

However, there were still no effective light cavalry forces in western Europe, except those of purely regional significance, such as in Scotland or Ireland. From the second half of the fifteenth century, the Venetian republic had recruited its light horsemen from among the Greeks and Albanians; these men were known as the stradiotti, and until the seventeenth century were ready to enter anybody's service. At the same time, the Hungarian hussar light horsemen appeared. The creation of light cavalry in the west was slowed by the knights' reluctance to part from their entourage, and their even greater dislike of changing from individual to collective combat. Development was also influenced by the advent of firearms. Mounted sharpshooters discarded the bow and crossbow in favour of the arquebus, one of the first firearms, and the first unit of mounted *arquebusiers* was formed in 1496 in Italy by Camillo Vitelli. From 1512 to the mid-sixteenth century, such horsemen were part of the French Compagnies d'Ordonnance, but comprised a separate group in battle. At the beginning of the seventeenth century, when the arquebus was replaced by the carbine, cavalrymen so armed became known as *carabiniers*.

France was one of the most progressive states of the time, and from the first half of the sixteenth century clearly differentiated the various kinds of cavalrymen. From 1549, there were also separate commanding bodies. The *gendarmerie*, heavy armoured horsemen, were commanded, in the king's name, by the *connteable*, while the colonel-general commanded the light cavalry. The organizational units known as lances gradually disappeared.

The transformation of cavalry accelerated in the second half of the century. In 1557, the first cornets, of 100 men each, were formed in England and were commanded by the general of cavalry, assisted by one lieutenant-general, one quartermaster-general, two commissaries and one provost-marshal.

In the wars among the German protestant dukes (1546–55), mercenary cavalrymen called *schwarze reitern* (black riders) took part. They were effective but undisciplined and prone to plundering. They were armed with pistols and swords – no longer spears – and used helmets and partial armour for protection. During the Wars of Religion (1562–98), formed in close order columns, they used new tactics – the caracole – which concentrated

English border horseman, sixteenth century

Mounted arquebusier, early seventeenth century

German cuirassier, 1630

maximum pistol fire against the heavily armoured knights. The new European cavalry was born from the clash of a line of riders armed with lances and a long column armed with pistols. The pistol emerged triumphant; its advantage was that it could be manipulated with one hand, the other being used to control the horse. It was not unknown for a pistol to fail to go off, which was why every man carried between two and six. Training to use a pistol also took less time than teaching a man to use the heavy lance, and smaller horses could be used by pistol-carrying units, as their armour was much lighter. On the other hand, the knights' armour, though improved and strengthened, could no longer withstand the increased penetration of the firearms deployed by the infantry and light cavalry. Towards the end of the sixteenth century, heavily armoured cavalrymen stopped using horse-armour, and reduced their own, becoming *cuirassiers*. The tactics of the reiters were adopted by all cavalry forces. Owing to improved weaponry and training, the depth of battle formation decreased first to ten lines, and towards the end of the century to six or seven. Shallower formations using the same number of men meant wider fronts, which had to be controlled by discipline and training. The cavalry of the period was therefore a modern force, acting as an organized troop.

The beginning of the seventeenth century saw several major conflicts. The Thirty Years War (1618–48) began as a religious war and turned into a clash between the feudal–Catholic reaction and the new social forces. The English Civil War (1642–8) saw a division along similar lines. Numerous armies crossed Europe, carrying new skills of war and tactical innovations, as well as the latest in weapons and equipment.

Cavalry made up nearly one-third of operational armies, and larger units had to be formed. In France, the basis was 4,000–5,000 semi-regular gendarmes and half-armoured pistoliers supported by a section of carabiniers, 1,000 men of the Cornete Blanche (volunteer noble force), 200 Guard *chevaux-legers*, and the gentlemen's unit of the Carabiniers du Roi, who in 1662 became the famous Grey Musketeers. In 1634, there were 98 cavalry squadrons, with 100 men each. The following year, regiments of two squadrons each were formed. Dragoons, who were classed as light cavalry, were formed into separate regiments.

In Sweden, a heavy cavalry regiment was made up of between one and three squadrons with two to six cornets each; in dragoon units, there were no cornets, but companies. Each of these numbered 125 men. In 1647, regiments of the imperial (Austrian) cavalry were divided into five squadrons, with ten companies – a total of 1,000 men. The regiment was commanded by a colonel (*oberst*) and lieutenant-colonel (*oberstleutnant*), and there were ten to fifteen men on the regimental staff.

In England, the Ironsides cavalry regiments of the New Model Army appeared in 1644, made up of six troops of 100 men each. Each regiment was commanded by a colonel, major and four captains, and also had a lieutenant, a cornet, a quartermaster and three trumpeters. Dragoon regiments had 10 companies of 100 men and two drummers.

From the beginning of the seventeenth century, heavy cavalry consisted of the cuirassiers. They mostly wore three-quarter armour, and were armed with two pistols and a straight thrusting sword. According to the standards of the Thirty Years War, riders protected by helmet and corselet (breastplate shot-proof, backplate pistol-proof), armed with pistols and a straight sword, were classed as light cavalry. In all armies, the light cavalry also consisted of carabiniers and dragoons, and some recruited light native horsemen from their border areas. The Austrian Empire used Croats and Hungarian hussars; Poles and Czechs availed themselves of the services of Cossacks; English armies included numerous Scottish 'border horse' troops.

Swedish King Gustavus II Adolphus (1611–32) introduced significant reforms into cavalry warfare. During the Thirty Years War, he perceived that caracoling was of no use against a cavalry force resolved to strike. His cavalry attacked with drawn swords and in formation only three lines deep, and pistols were used only as auxiliary weapons during the mêlée. Only men of the first line were allowed to fire one shot, then the attack proceeded with cold steel. To ensure adequate support for his cavalry charges, Gustavus placed small musketeer units between his squadrons, and gave each regiment two light cannon. They were also successful at operational reconnaissance and, at moments of crises, successive charges made possible the withdrawal of infantry and artillery. After the Battle of Lützen (1632), the imperial cavalry also abandoned the caracole, and adopted the Swedish idea of musketeers providing fire support from positions in the cavalry formation. Somewhat later, France also abolished the caracole.

In the general battle disposition, infantry took up the centre in chess-board formation, and the main cavalry forces were deployed on one wing or both wings. At the Battle of Breitenfeld (1631), imperial forces under Pappenheim grouped 5,000 cavalry on the left wing, and six times charged unsuccessfully the Swedish right wing, but in the largest battles of the Thirty Years War, cavalry masses began to play decisive roles. In one of the bloodiest, again at Breitenfeld (1642), 10,000 Swedish cavalry clashed with 16,000 imperial horsemen. In the English Civil War, Cromwell organized 11 regiments of highly disciplined riders in a mobile reserve; at Naseby (1645), he placed it on the wings of his formation, facing the royalists, and this decided the outcome of the fateful battle.

RENAISSANCE OF THE COLD STEEL STRIKE,
1650–1800

As the absolutist monarchies opted for the creation of standing armies, cavalry was increasingly assigned the role of principal manoeuvring force, while the infantry continued with rigid linear tactics. The ratio of cavalry to infantry was anywhere from 1:6 to 1:3; it was still divided into light and heavy, but the distinction was now mainly in tactics, not in equipment or armament. Heavy cavalry was used in combat, while reconnaissance, security, pursuit, raids and skirmishes were reserved for the light. In wartime, larger units – brigades – were formed, and towards the end of the nineteenth century, even divisions. Because of increasingly accurate firepower, cavalry had to move more quickly on the battlefield, so the strike with drawn swords, in full gallop, was gradually adopted. The depth of the attacking formation was decreased to achieve greater effect.

The heavy and light cavalry became specialized for particular tasks. The heavy included cuirassiers, dragoons, carabiniers, horse grenadiers,

Swedish trooper of Charles XI, end of seventeenth century

Austrian cuirassier, 1700

regiments of horse, as well as the chevaux-legers of France, although their name denotes precisely the opposite – light cavalry. Hussars, uhlans, lancers, chasseurs, mounted jägers, light dragoons, Bosniaks and Cossacks belonged to the light cavalry. In some states they were regular units, in others irregular troops. Cuirassiers were armed with a straight sword, two pistols and a carbine, and wore breastplates for protection, but towards the end of the eighteenth century, Prussian, Russian and Swedish cuirassiers abandoned armour altogether. Dragoons stopped being mounted infantry, and became cavalry trained to fight on foot, and were therefore included in the medium cavalry in some countries. Besides a sword or sabre, they had two pistols and a carbine or musket with bayonet; from 1702 Swedish dragoons also used hand grenades. Carabiniers and grenadiers were similar, but the former usually had carbines without bayonets, while the latter used hand grenades and muskets with bayonets. Hussars usually had a curved sabre, pistols and a carbine, while chasseurs and jägers used a rifle with bayonet. Uhlans, lancers, Cossacks and Bosniaks also had spears and lances.

The troop or company remained the basic formation, numbering from 30 to 100; the squadron became an administrative and tactical unit of 100–200 men, usually divided into two troops. Regiments consisted of four to ten squadrons, but units larger than this began to be created. From 1657, the French army, both in war and on manoeuvres, had a group of two to four regiments under the command of a *brigadier de cavalerie*. Similar formations in Russia were commanded by a major-general or brigadier, and after the Seven Years War (1756–63), two-regiment brigades became standing units in both France and Russia. Guard cavalry became battle units, and horse artillery was created.

The example of Gustavus II Adolphus was at first followed only by the English Protectorate (1649–69). Well-trained and highly disciplined, it used a two-line formation, and charged at a gallop. The second line backed the first if necessary, or attacked the flanks and rear of the enemy. In other cavalry forces, notably the Prussian, mounted firepower was again favoured over the cold steel attack. Charges were executed at a trot or short gallop, so their effect was weak. Because of insufficient training, Russian cavalry of the mid-seventeenth century would break formation during the charge, so they preferred to receive the enemy attack with a salvo from horseback; the dragoons would dismount and form a square. The Austrians continued to discharge a pistol salvo prior to the charge as late as the second half of that century, and when fighting the Turkish cavalry, they dismounted and fired from a square, like infantry.

In the eighteenth century, the charge with drawn swords again prevailed over firearms. Charles XII of Sweden (1697–1718), realizing the importance of speed, and emulating the French cavalry under the command of the Prince de Condé, ordered the charge with drawn steel in the Swedish cavalry, the use of firearms being allowed only in rare circumstances. During the War of the Spanish Succession (1701–14) the English commander, the Duke of Marlborough, created great cavalry masses, sometimes up to 100 squadrons in strength, which he used as a mobile reserve in the decisive moments of a battle. He allowed his cavalrymen to hold firearms only when on guard duty; charges were executed exclusively with cold steel. Eugène of Savoy was also a supporter of full-tilt charges, but could not realize his ideas in the Austrian forces.

Prussian cavalry was weak, slow and inefficient, and suffered repeated defeats by the Austrians during the War of the Austrian Succession (1740–8). Frederick II (1740–86) reorganized it; foreigners were no longer allowed to serve, and capable commanders such as von Ziethen and von Seydlitz were appointed. Many new rules and commands turned it into an effective fighting force. As soon as the enemy was sighted, a charge (*en échiquiers*) was ordered from a distance of 700 m/760 yds; in 1755, this was increased to 1,800 m/2,000 yds. At 200 m/220 yds, the men were to change to full gallop, with swords drawn, flags unfurled, and as much noise as possible made by shouting and trumpets. Firing from horseback was not allowed. The battle order was made up of three lines, each with men in three ranks; the first was made up of cuirassiers, the second, 300 paces behind, of dragoons, and the third, protecting the flanks and rear, of hussars. From 1770, the second line used a tapering formation, so there was no further need for the third. After the 1755 reforms, the Russian cavalry also charged with cold steel, and firing from pistols or carbines was allowed for heavy cavalry only when opposed with skirmishing light cavalry. Regiments' battle formation was in two lines; the central squadrons were in ranks, and the wing squadrons in files. When having to beat back the charge of a superior mounted force, a regiment could form a square; in this case, the men were allowed to dismount. After the Seven Years War, other armies also abolished firing from horseback. Gallop charges were not introduced in France until 1776.

In the general order of battle, cavalry was usually at the wings of the infantry, so as not to interfere with their line of fire and to protect the wings and flanks. When advancing, it moved at the infantry's speed and could not peel away to attack the opposing cavalry until it was at 500 m/550 yds; the tendency, of course, was to do this as early as possible, so as not to suffer unnecessarily from enemy artillery. After a successful attack, several squadrons would pursue the enemy troopers, while the rest would attack the flanks and rear of the opposing infantry. Sometimes, if the cavalry attack was very successful, all the mounted troops would give chase, and would not appear again on the battlefield.

During the Siege of Vienna in 1683, Polish King Jan Sobieski, heading a force of 26,000 men, defeated numerically superior Turkish forces. The main strike was delivered by the Poles on the right wing, as their cavalry was the most numerous: 3,000 winged hussars, 8,000 pancerni, 2,000 light cavalry, 2,000 dragoons, 500 reiters and 300 Cossacks. At Blenheim (1704), 86 squadrons of British and Allied cavalry routed nine French infantry battalions and 30 squadrons of cavalry. At Malplaquet (1709), a fierce cavalry battle developed, with changing luck; 260 French squadrons were pitted against 300 Allied squadrons. Finally, the British cavalry broke through the French battle order, and the French were forced to execute a general retreat. Charles XII realized that mixing cavalry and infantry was not viable, and abolished this practice in the Swedish army, where cavalry became the main core of the military. They attacked infantry, batteries, even fortifications, and decided the outcome of battles practically alone. The cavalry of Frederick II attacked *en masse*, and was a first-class manoeuvring and striking force. At Rossbach (1757) it broke the imperial cavalry, then struck the French infantry with a charge on the right flank. It lost 550 men, the enemy 10,000! At Leuthen the same year, it defeated the Austrian

Austrian hussar officer, 1750

Hanover dragoon, 1760

cavalry, which, retreating, caused panic among its infantry. At the Battle of Zorndorf (1758), the Russian cavalry twice broke the formation of Prussian infantry, but was twice forced back by strong counter-charges of the superior Prussian cavalry. The cavalry of the Russian commander Count Suvorov was not in the same class, but at Kinburn, in 1787, it rode into the sea, taking advantage of the shallow water, and outflanked the Turks; the next year, it charged the forts of Riminiku-Serata and Ismail, the latter dismounted.

This period saw the more intensive use of cavalry for reconnaissance, skirmishes and pursuit. Oliver Cromwell used to send his cavalry out for a whole day's reconnaissance; French Marshal Henri Turenne used units of 50 men, and Austrian hussars proved particularly successful scouts in the war with Prussia. They circled the Prussian army, harassing it constantly, following its staff units, capturing couriers, while screening the grouping of their own army and masking its intentions. They also threatened enemy lines of communication and attacked small units in the Prussians' rear. At the head of 4,000 hussars, with four cannon, Austrian General Haddick captured Berlin for two days in 1757. After a convoy headed for Olmütz was captured, the Prussian army had to lift its siege of the town, and leave Bohemia. During the Seven Years War, Cossacks created an impenetrable screen in front of the Russian army.

Pursuit was an increasingly common practice in all armies. After the victory at Preston (1648), Cromwell's forces pursued the enemy for three days and nights, and after Kunersdorf (1759), the defeated Prussian cavalry was pursued first by the enemy's regular units and then by the hussars and Cossacks. Even though he did not approve of the practice at first, Frederick II sent Ziethen in pursuit, at the head of 55 squadrons, after the Battle of Leuthen, and later, in the instructions of 1788, he demanded energetic and merciless pursuit from his cavalry until the enemy was destroyed.

The first modern cavalry rules were published in France in 1720: *Le service ordinaire de la cavalerie*. Similar rules soon appeared in Prussia and other states, but organized training was begun only by Frederick. It included individual training, group training with special assignments on difficult ground and drilling in moving, manoeuvring and managing large cavalry masses. Schools for riding instruction were formed. After the Seven Years War, other countries introduced systematic training according to the Prussian model. In France, the Duc de Choiseul introduced a permanent officer corps, and set up troop breeding stables, so commanders would no longer oppose training on the grounds that it exhausted their horses. He founded one veterinary and six riding schools, but after his death only one remained, at Saumur. The first rule-book for the training of the French cavalry, *Ordonnance*, was published in 1776; it mainly adopted Prussian tactics. The rules of 1788 decreed the abolition of companies in favour of divisions of two troops; two divisions made up a squadron. There were also regulations concerning the formation of a regiment, the training of individuals and squadrons, movement and charge; additional parts dealt specifically with dragoons, hussars, and so on. Charges were to be executed in line, in echelons when the intention was to pierce an enemy formation, in tapering formation when the aim was to outflank, and in columns when the object of the attack was the infantry. The Austrian rules were published by Marshal Lassy: shooting from horseback was to be used only against the

Turks; after a successful charge, the units regrouped; pursuit was conducted by one corporal and eight men from each wing of the squadron.

Austrian general and military writer Montecuccoli considered the spear queen of weapons, and thought that cavalrymen should be armoured and formed in regiments of 750 men. The battle order was to be a squadron in three ranks; cuirassiers were to make up the centre, in two lines, and the dragoons the wings. French Marshal de Saxe also thought the spear should be the principal weapon of the cavalry whom he divided into two groups: cuirassiers and dragoons. The cuirassiers' role was to strike, the dragoons' – everything else. He also thought that cavalrymen should be of low stature, intelligent and dextrous, and pointed out the importance of systematic training for keeping in peak form: 2,000 paces trotting, without tiring. In Great Britain, Captain Hinde published his *Discipline of the Light Horse* in 1778, in which he suggested training and combat procedures in many ways ahead of their time.

THE 'MODERN' AGE, 1800–1900

At the beginning of the Revolutionary Wars in 1792, the French cavalry was weakened by the disintegration of the royal army. Renewal was difficult, because no trained personnel or horses were available. All the cavalry was transformed into light units, although the regiments kept their former names, but divided among the combined units, the cavalry was barely noticeable on the battlefield.

A decree of 1793 ordered the forming of 29 regiments of heavy cavalry, 20 of dragoons, 23 of chasseurs and 11 of hussars. Regiments consisted of four to six squadrons of varying strengths; in all, these had about 440 squadrons with 50,000 men. Cavalry regiments, or brigades consisting of two regiments, formed part of infantry divisions. The first such division, albeit temporary, was created by General Jourdan, from cavalry taken from the infantry divisions of the armies of Sambre and Meuse. General Hoche did the same in 1797 and, from then on, the presence of the French cavalry began to be felt on the battlefield. At Marengo (1800) two cavalry brigades contributed to the victory by their charge against the Austrian infantry. Napoleon transformed eight cavalry regiments into cuirassiers, supplying them with breastplates, and at the beginning of the Napoleonic Wars (1804–15) a fifth squadron was added to the regiments. Permanent war formations were decided in 1805, the same year as the cavalry reserve under Marshal Murat was formed. It was made up of two divisions of cuirassiers, five of dragoons and several independent brigades of light cavalry. Each division had one or two batteries of horse artillery.

At the beginning of the nineteenth century, there were four basic types of cavalry, although distinctions were not closely observed in some armies. The **heavy cavalry** consisted of cuirassiers, carabiniers and some guard regiments which traditionally had different names (Royal Horse Guards, Life Guards, Gardes du Corps, Chevaliers-Gardes). Its role was to break the opposing cavalry force and create an opportunity to support its own infantry. Because of their weight, and the types of horses they rode, cuirassiers and carabiniers could not move fast and far. They therefore took

French carabinier, 1812

Swedish officer, dragoons, 1806

Officer, French Guard Chasseurs, 1805

up positions behind the lines, and awaited the signal for a mass charge.

The **medium cavalry** consisted of the dragoons, whose versatility made them the most numerous of the cavalry troops. When firearms appeared, an infantryman placed on a horse became a dragoon, and in time, dragoons became cavalrymen trained to fight on foot. They were trained to fight both as heavy cavalry and to scout as light cavalry. However, they did not have the striking force of the cuirassiers, the speed and mobility of the light cavalry or the firepower of the infantry. It was in this class that the differences among the various armies were most apparent; armies which did not have heavy cavalry used dragoons as battle cavalry.

Reconnaissance, patrolling, pursuit of the enemy, cutting lines of communication, capturing and securing inhabited fortifications, bridges and other important positions were all tasks of the **light cavalry**, which included the hussars, chevaux-legers, chasseurs, mounted jägers and light dragoons.

Finally, the fourth type, also classed as light, combined the speed of light cavalry and the striking impact of the heavy cavalry: these were the **light cavalrymen armed with spears and lances** – uhlans, lancers and Cossacks.

In France at the beginning of the nineteenth century, a cuirassier's horse cost about 300 francs, a dragoon's 200, and that of a light cavalryman about 100. Especially good horses, for officers or guard units, cost 500 francs or more. In Austria, the equipping of a mounted jäger cost 2,200 crowns, a hussar 2,800 and a cuirassier 3,300 crowns. By comparison, equipping an infantryman cost 200.

In the order of battle, cavalry was on the wings or in the centre, ready for action. At Austerlitz (1805), the cavalry reserve distinguished itself in charges against General Bagration's 5th column. At Eylau (1807) 80 squadrons formed in a massive brigade column struck at the Russian infantry in front of the centre of the French position.

After the defeat of Austria in 1805 and Prussia in 1806, French cavalry acquired a number of good horses, and was also strengthened by the excellent riders of the Confederation of the Rhine (German states) and the Duchy of Warsaw (Poland). Light lancer regiments were formed of these Polish troops, modelled on the Austrian uhlans. At Eckmül (1809), in the largest cavalry battle of the Napoleonic Wars, the French cuirassiers, in fierce and persistent combat, routed the Austrian cuirassiers and dragoons, and at Wagram, the same year, the charge of guard cavalry and cuirassiers facilitated the infantry's penetration of the centre. In mid-1812, before the invasion of Russia, Napoleon's cavalry numbered 95,000 men and some regiments had up to six squadrons. Each of ten army corps had a light cavalry division with 2,500 men, the guard had 2,600 men, and the associated Austrian corps 7,300. The main body was made up of the cavalry reserve, which consisted of four corps with about 40,000 men and 114 cannon. At Borodino, the French, by repeated infantry and cavalry charges, captured the Raevsky battery, the centre of the Russian position, despite strong resistance and a counter-attack by the Russian cavalry.

However, it was in Russia that the French were completely destroyed. By the spring of 1813, Napoleon could barely scrape together 5,000 cavalrymen for operations in Germany, and only 40,000 by the autumn, and regiments were reduced to four squadrons each. Although this new force never became the equal of its predecessor, it could be effective. At Mormant (1814), the cavalry corps of Milhaud and Kellerman, consisting of three dragoon divisions and one light, executed a surprise attack on the Russian corps of General Phalen, which included one infantry, one cavalry and one Cossack division, and vanquished it after a series of charges, then gave pursuit, capturing several battalions and cannon. But by 1815, the cavalry reserve had only 14,000 men in four corps, and at the Battle of Waterloo the massed French charges met the firm wall of British infantry and artillery.

The tactics used by the French cavalry were simple: charge was ordered as soon as a favourable position relative to the enemy was achieved. Only when faced with a superior cavalry force did the French resort to flanking. Insufficiently trained, the French usually executed charges at a trot, and Waterloo was one of the rare instances when they charged at full gallop. The battle order consisted of masses in deep echelons, with a front of squadron or regiment width. This was not an expression of new tactics, but reflected the inability of the poorly trained lower units to operate independently. Squadrons, regiments, even brigades were formed up one behind the other, so the attack resembled a series of repeated charges.

In war, the role of cavalry was to secure, reconnoitre and pursue. During the advance on Leipzig in 1806, the vanguard, under Murat, consisted of three brigades of light cavalry and two divisions of dragoons. In the Ulm operations of 1805, Murat's cavalry executed a successful diversion on the Rhine, then secured the flank of the advancing army. Strategic reconnoitring was carried out by the reserve, using a widespread network of squads, squadrons and patrols of light cavalry, supported by a strong main force of up to four regiments. After 1812, it was no longer used for strategic reconnoitring; it was deemed advisable to conserve its strength for the battles. But, while it was still at the peak of its power, it played the main part in strategic pursuit, for which the main requirements were speed, energy and tenacity. The most effective of these operations was after the Battle of Jena (1806) when Murat's cavalry covered 35 km/22 miles daily for several weeks, exerting constant pressure on retreating Prussian columns.

Towards the end of the eighteenth century Austrian, Russian and Prussian cavalry increasingly became part of infantry divisions and corps as auxiliary troops, which is why Prussian and Russian cuirassiers discarded their armour, a hindrance in their new tasks. In the battles of 1805 to 1807 the Prussians, Russians and Austrians were unable to gather sufficient mass to face the French cavalry reserve, and were defeated one after the other. A Russian army corps consisted of five or six infantry regiments, one each of cuirassiers, dragoons and hussars, and two regiments of Cossacks. The Prussian army was similarly organized.

Having experienced the superiority of the French, the Russians formed two cuirassier divisions in 1811. The rest of the cavalry was divided into corps, each consisting of four regiments of dragoons, one of hussars and one of uhlans. They also formed three Cossack corps with between nine and fourteen regiments each.

Prussia, Austria and Britain formed cavalry corps in 1814, but did not use them to create independent forces under one commander. They parcelled them out among various armies, which limited their operational and tactical possibilities. At Leipzig in 1813, the Allies had 60,000 cavalrymen, but could not organize effective pursuit of the defeated French.

Reconnoitring, flanking and skirmishing were the specialities of the

Cossacks. They shadowed the retreating French army in 1812, executing raids and capturing any who left the column, thus hastening the demise of the Grande Armée. At the beginning of 1813, 3,000 Cossacks, detached over 350 km/220 miles in advance of the front, executed a raid on Berlin.

Views on the use of cavalry did not change significantly after 1815. Prominent military writers still ascribed to it a role similar to the one it had at the time of Napoleon. Clausewitz considered it to be the branch of the military best suited to movement and large-scale solutions, especially on spacious battlefields and when great decisive blows were planned (his thinking was not influenced by the development of firearms). In attacking well-defended positions, it needed the support of infantry and artillery; alone, it could achieve success only against infantry already in combat. Mass cavalry charges were suitable against enemy cavalry and batteries, or as support for infantry taking a position.

Cavalry weapons had not changed much either in the middle of the nineteenth century. Swords or sabres, pistols and carbines were the principal weapons of all mounted soldiers. Particular horsemen used lances, and dragoons had bayonets. In the second half of the century, nearly all cavalry was armed with short rifles or carbines. Cuirassiers kept their breastplates, although they no longer offered any protection from firearms. Cavalry was still divided into heavy, line and light, but this was no longer founded on weight but on differences in armament. Dragoons were equally likely to be found in heavy, line or light cavalry in various countries. In peacetime cavalry was organized in regiments of four to ten squadrons of decreased strength; brigades, divisions or corps existed only in Russia.

During the American Civil War (1861–5) most of the Confederate (Southern) cavalry were organized in brigades, divisions and corps and constituted an independent force. The Union (Northern) cavalry was part of infantry brigades, and in the first two years of the war was consistently defeated. In 1863, a Cavalry Corps, three divisions strong, was formed under General Stoneman. Completely on his own, at the head of 9,000 troopers, he clashed with a weaker Confederate force in the largest cavalry battle of the war – Brandy Station.

All American cavalry was armed with carbines and revolvers; some Union regiments had lances, and from 1864, Union troopers were armed with seven-shot Spencer carbines. Infantry, armed with rifles, and artillery, also using rifled weapons, had increasing firepower, and the cavalry soon realized that the period of great charges was past, and learned to fight on foot. Charges were reserved for clashes with opposing cavalry, but even in hand-to-hand fighting the revolver was favoured over the sabre. Manoeuvres with large cavalry units and raids behind the enemy lines were successfully executed. General J.E.B. Stuart, at the head of 1,200 Confederate raiders, encircled the whole Union army for three days in June 1862, lost only one man, and brought back 165 prisoners and valuable information. Besides intelligence gathering, raids served the purpose of destroying vital enemy centres of transport and communication. General Morgan, leading 3,900 Confederate troopers and with one battery, destroyed railway junctions and bridges from Nashville to Louisville, captured Elizabethtown, and brought back 2,000 prisoners and many horses, losing only 66 men. In May 1864, Union General Sheridan conducted the largest raid of the war thus far, taking 10,000 troopers behind enemy lines for a whole month, and in April

Union cavalryman, 1861–5

1865, the South was defeated at Five Forks because Sheridan had encircled their position and cut their lines of communication.

In the Austro-Prussian War of 1866, the Prussians had only one cavalry corps, 14 regiments in strength, and a reserve of seven regiments. The rest was in infantry units. Austrian infantry corps, four to five brigades strong, had one cavalry regiment, which gave one of its squadrons to each brigade. The rest – 28 regiments – was in the reserve. The lessons of the American Civil War had not been learned: it was still thought that European cavalry should follow the old rules and charge with drawn steel. Because of wrong perceptions and use, cavalry had little effect. In the Bohemian theatre, cavalry masses moved behind the front lines, while the Austrians used only one light division for reconnaissance. The Prussians used their divisional cavalry for this task. Cavalry did not intervene at the critical moments, because it was behind the front lines. Only at the Battle of Königgrätz (Sadowa) when the Austrian army was forced to retreat, was part of the Prussian cavalry detached for pursuit, but two Austrian divisions – 12 regiments – broke the Prussian cavalry with a series of charges, and secured the withdrawal of the main force. The Austrians had more success in the Italian theatre, by creating an impenetrable screen for its army and charging enemy infantry. At Villafranca, two cavalry brigades charged the squares of two Italian infantry divisions. They lost nearly half their men, but the Italians were tied down for the whole day and could not take part in the decisive moments of the Battle of Custozza.

In the Franco-Prussian War (1870–1), the Prussian cavalry organization was similar to that of 1866, whereas the French had independent cavalry divisions. Prussian cavalry carried out wide reconnaissance through a network of patrols, but often did not fan out far enough from its troops. For example, two cavalry divisions of the 2nd Army were detached four days' march in advance; when they made contact with the enemy, they were only 5 km/3 miles out; and, on the day of the Battle of Vert, they were deep behind the front line, so could not be used to pursue the defeated enemy. The French cavalry, ineptly commanded, moved only in divisional masses, and was reserved for battles, as Napoleon had done with his cavalry reserve. It carried out only close reconnaissance, so the French were nearly always surprised by the appearance of the Prussians. In battle, especially at moments of crisis, the cavalry charged against infantry and artillery with many losses but little effect. At Mars-la-Tour, the French cuirassiers of the Guard lost half their men in a charge against the Prussian 10th Infantry Brigade. Immediately afterwards, the French infantry repulsed a charge by the strengthened Prussian 6th Cavalry Division, inflicting severe losses, and broke it in a repeated charge, although its first line had been penetrated. The only partial cavalry success was achieved by the 12th Cavalry Brigade of General von Bredow, but at the cost of many lives: the Prussians later called this the *todesritt* (death ride). They held back the French infantry, and forced the artillery to change position, thus enabling the Prussian 20th Infantry Division to withdraw.

The forming of divisions only in wartime did not turn out to be a good idea, because the commanders involved did not know their troops well enough and these were not trained for combat in divisional formation. In 1873, France introduced peacetime divisions, which filled the need for training and could be used for border protection. Other armies followed

Cossack of the Russian Imperial Guard, 1900

Sergeant, Bengal Cavalry, 1908

suit. These divisions consisted of two to three brigades, usually with two regiments of four squadrons each. They also included engineering, communications and medical detachments, and in Great Britain a bridge-building team. Gradually, all cavalry units were trained to fight on foot, turning into dragoons, although the old names – cuirassiers, hussars, uhlans – were retained. Sabres and carbines became the universal weapons. Although cavalry suffered heavy casualties from firearms in the Franco-Prussian War, and achieved very little, it was still believed that it could have an important role in warfare if adequate changes in tactics were made and it was put to more purposeful use. French cavalry rules of 1876 foresaw cavalry being used for direct attacks, for flanking attacks, and as a reserve. Divisions should therefore be drawn in three lines, by brigades: the rear lines would support the front, increasing the strength of the strike, shoring up the flanks, or serving as a reserve. Instructions provided for reconnaissance cavalry to move in the same formation: the first line would make contact with the enemy and puncture his security screen, the second would provide back-up, and the third would be a reserve. Infantry divisions in France were assigned one regiment of cavalry, in Germany a squadron, in Austro-Hungary and Japan three squadrons, and in Russia from one squadron to one regiment of Cossacks.

In the Russo-Turkish War of 1877–8, the Russians did not have an independent cavalry force, and had to form scouting units from elements of their corps cavalry. Detached from their formation units, they did not do a good job of reconnoitring. A mass of 80 squadrons, also assembled from various units, tried vainly to blockade Pleven. Because of heavy fire, cavalry fought mostly on foot; operations on horseback were allowed only in exceptionally favourable circumstances. A typical case was at the Battle of Lovec: the Black Sea Cossack Brigade supported the infantry charge on foot, then mounted to give chase to the enemy, and destroyed Turkish reserves of six battalions in a surprise attack.

In the United States, after the end of the Civil War, the cavalry was frequently engaged in fighting the numerous Indian tribes; this mostly took the form of a series of small clashes and skirmishes. In 1876, units of the US Cavalry under the command of General Custer suffered their worst defeat at the hands of the united Sioux and Cheyenne tribes at Little Big Horn.

Towards the end of the nineteenth century cavalry armament was partially modified after the introduction of firearms with greater rates of fire. Spears were still used by the Cossacks in Russia, the lancers in Great Britain and the uhlans in Germany and Austro-Hungary. Cuirassiers' breastplates were abolished in Austro-Hungary in 1881, and from 1888 were used only for parades in Germany. France discontinued their use in 1880, but reintroduced them in 1883. However, there were no significant changes in the tactics and use of the cavalry. German rules of 1886 still considered the charge the basic mode of operation, and prescribed the three-line formation. The British cavalry set its own standards, conditioned by its activities against indigenous forces in Africa and Asia which still fought in traditional ways.

The appearance of machine-guns and rapid-fire artillery further limited the use of cavalry. In the South African (Boer) War (1899–1902), Great Britain used 18 cavalry regiments, which fought on foot most of the time. On the other hand, the Boers, using fast horses adapted to the local climate, mounted very successful guerrilla operations. Only once did the British undertake a large-scale cavalry operation: in February 1900, in the relief of the besieged town of Kimberley, a cavalry division 3,000 men strong took part, under the command of Sir John French, and backed by seven batteries of horse artillery was the largest cavalry force fielded since the Battle of Waterloo. Because of the nature of operations in the Boer War, the British army also used the services of about 10,000 yeomanry mounted infantrymen. After the war, the lance was dropped from the cavalry's armament, but was brought back in 1914.

In the Russo-Japanese War of 1904–5, sheer firepower precluded mounted operations, and the Russian cavalry did not have much success in reconnaissance either. Its reports on the enemy and his intentions were sketchy, and even the Cossack raids of General Mishchenko were unsuccessful, because they were slackly conducted, the Cossacks retreating as soon as they encountered infantry fire. The Japanese cavalry, although inferior to western European cavalry, carried through scouting operations with more precision and stood up well to the Russian Cossacks, especially in hand-to-hand fighting with sabres. At the Battle of Sha-ho (1904) the Japanese made several charges on the Russian positions with cavalry brigade strength.

Although wars had shown that the time of great cavalry charges was past, and that cavalry had to fight mainly on foot, European armies stubbornly stuck to the view that combat on horseback was still primary. German cavalry rules of 1910 continued to treat mounted operations as the principal mode of combat, mainly against enemy cavalry but also against infantry and artillery, provided that the element of surprise was exploited. The rules declared that, in defensive operations, cavalry could temporarily defend inhabited positions, but had to take care to protect its sides, lest the enemy attack from behind with a flanking manoeuvre.

Spahy trooper from Senegal, 1910

EPILOGUE

Mobilization prior to World War I (1914–18) put an unprecedented number of men into the saddle. Cavalry had reached the apogee of its development: never before had it been better equipped or boasted better horses than at the beginning of the twentieth century. However, its direct rival – infantry – had advanced much further, and new competitors had appeared: tanks and aeroplanes. In the end cavalry had its grand finale after the show was over.

At the beginning of the war, the independent cavalry divisions of the warring parties were: 10 French, 11 German, 11 Austro-Hungarian, 36 Russian, two Turkish, one British, one Belgian, one Bulgarian and one Serbian. On the Western Front, Germany had 144 active and reserve regiments with 552 squadrons, France 131 regiments with 550 squadrons, Great Britain 31 regiments with 124 squadrons and Belgium seven regiments with 28 squadrons; in all, 1,254 squadrons, with over 110,000 men. India sent 15 cavalry regiments to Europe. On the Eastern Front the Russians alone had 150,000 Cossacks in six armies and about 60,000 men in 71 regular regiments.

Nearly half a million cavalrymen rode off to war, and were met with machine-guns, rapid-fire cannon, poison gas, barbed wire and trenches. They dismounted, abandoned their horses, and continued the war on foot.

Polish Uhlan of 7th Regiment, 1939

1
Assyrian Horse Archer

seventh century BC

Three thousand years ago, riding and controlling a horse without benefit of stirrups or saddle, and with just a primitive bridle, was a military problem in itself, and a complex one at that. Riders rode bareback, sitting towards the back of the horse, with legs raised rather high. They could not lower them because of the breadth of the horse's belly. This position was extremely unstable, so the reins had to be short and rather stiff, as they served not only to direct the horse but for holding on. For that reason, too, the bits were wider on the sides, so the rider wouldn't pull them out if he grabbed the bridle too tightly. It is likely that after prolonged use this type of bridle caused wounds to the horses' mouths.

A lot of information on the character and appearance of the Assyrian riders can be gathered from the remains of stone reliefs, the most famous of which are found in the ruins of Nimrod, Khorsabad and Nineveh.

From the beginning of the ninth to the end of the seventh century BC, three phases of development of the Assyrian cavalry can be discerned, which seem to be connected with three well-known rulers.

Reliefs from the time of King Assurnasirapli II (883–59BC) show light, unarmoured archers, some of whom are leading two horses, which lends credence to the theory that these horses lacked stamina and riders had to change mounts frequently. Also shown are pairs of riders; one of them is shooting an arrow, and the other handling both horses. In the ninth century BC, Assyrian horsemen had an auxiliary role, and their principal mode of combat was with bows and arrows or throwing javelins.

By the time of King Tiglathpileser III (745–27BC), the Assyrian horse archers are partially armoured: evidence that their tactics in battle were more aggressive, and that their role had increased in importance.

Finally, during the reign of King Assurbarnapal (668–26BC) there were three kinds of horsemen in the Assyrian army; light riders (members of nomadic tribes under Assyrian powers armed with bows and javelins), heavy archers in scale armour, and even more stoutly armoured riders, shown in close lance and sword combat with enemy heavy infantry.

As the cavalry became increasingly important, and gained the upper hand over combat chariots, the chariots became more and more weighty, and finally turned into a combination of battle platform and transport for heavy infantry, drawn by four horses.

During the period when we know of the Assyrian cavalry, the equipment of riders and horses became richer and more ornate. Riding gained in status, whereas it had been considered vulgar. Kings, the nobility and elite warriors used combat chariots driven by somebody else. One had to do the riding oneself.

The picture shows an Assyrian archer of the late period, on a horse 14 hands (145 cm/58 in) tall. The colour of the horse is that of the very old Akhal-Teke breed, now cultivated in Turkmenia, and closely related to the old Iranian breeds.

ASSYRIAN HORSE ARCHER
seventh century BC

2
Phrygian
Heavy Cavalryman
fifth century BC

The continents of Asia and Europe are connected by the 'bridge' known as Asia Minor, or, in modern Turkey, Anatolia. This rolling and fertile area was the path taken by barbarian tribes who came from the north, some of whom certainly contributed to the downfall of the Hittite kingdom. About 800BC, a people called the Phrygians set up their kingdom in Anatolia, which later became the Lydian kingdom.

The country was rich, and the inhabitants made good use of its gifts, including minerals. Electrum, an alloy of gold and silver, was known to the Lydians, who found it in the river Pactolus, and used this 'white gold' to make the first coins we know of. The invention of money facilitated trade, and Lydia became an extremely rich and powerful country, especially after the fall of Assyria around 612BC. Even today, we say 'rich as Croesus', during whose rule (560–46BC) Lydia was at the pinnacle of its power. It subjugated almost all the Greek cities of Asia Minor and captured Cappadocia in the east.

In 547BC, the opposing armies of Lydia, led by King Croesus, and the Persian Empire, under Emperor Cyrus II, fought at Pteria. After the battle, Croesus sent messengers to consult the Greek oracle at Delphi. The oracle said a great empire was to fall, and Croesus arrogantly assumed that the Persian Empire was headed for destruction. He began meticulous preparations for war, but while he was still about them the supposedly doomed Cyrus invaded Lydia, captured Sardis, the capital, and annexed the country.

Persia set up several provinces in the conquered areas of Asia Minor, including one named Phrygia. In the past two centuries archaeological excavations have been made in this former Persian province, and have yielded ample evidence of the quondam glory of Lydia and Phrygia. Several handsome depictions of warriors were preserved on carvings, vases and earthenware of the sixth and fifth centuries BC. The helmets and shields of horsemen were particularly ornate, and were probably used by the nobility. This type of protective equipment was later simply called 'Phrygian'. Croesus retained large numbers of mercenaries from Greek cities all over the Mediterranean, and Grecian influence in equipment and weaponry is evident.

There is hardly any data on the social status of warriors, their numbers or their strategy and tactics. A reasonable surmise is that the heavy cavalry was made up of the middle and high nobility, and the infantry by the Greeks, as was later the case under the Persians.

PHRYGIAN HEAVY CAVALRYMAN
fifth century BC

3
Persian Extra-heavy Cavalryman

fourth century BC

The epitaph on the tomb of King Darius I (522–486BC) reads: 'I was a great rider and a great hunter, for me nothing was impossible'. It is inconceivable that a ruler of a few centuries before would have wanted that inscription on his tomb, but cavalry had gained in status and even kings had started to ride. Hunting remained one of the main pleasures of the nobility, and to hunt with bow in the Iranian steppes one had to ride well; this was another source of good horsemen for the Persian cavalry.

The traditional weapon of the Iranian steppe nomads, the bow, was the main weapon of the light cavalry, while the heavy cavalry carried two or three iron-tipped javelins and a short sword. After the wars against the Greeks, in the fifth century BC, larger spears 3 m/10 ft long also came into use.

After the death of Darius II, his son Cyrus the Younger, satrap of Lydia, Phrygia, Cappadocia and commander of Persian forces in Asia Minor, disputed the right of succession of his brother Artaxerxes. In 401BC, he marched from Sardis, with a force of 13,000 Greek mercenary infantry, 2,600 cavalry and an unknown number of Persian infantry. Artaxerxes waited for him at Cunaxa, north-east of Babylon, with 6,000 cavalry and 30,000 infantry. The battle was started by the Greeks, who put Artaxerxes's left wing to flight without combat. The rest of Cyrus's army entered the fray, and Artaxerxes's right crumbled. Cyrus, at the head of 600 chosen horsemen, charged the remainder – 6,000 cavalry who stayed on the field.

The fierceness of the onslaught surprised the enemy and enabled Cyrus to break through at the head of a group of men and kill the commander of the enemy cavalry, Artagerses. He wounded his brother, but was himself slain by a javelin blow to the head. As his death solved the disputed succession, the battle stopped.

The Greek mercenaries were left without an employer, and their officers were treacherously killed. They were forced to retreat under constant attack from the Persian cavalry, and 6,000 of them succeeded in breaking through to the Black Sea. Known as 'The retreat of the ten thousand', this demonstrated the superiority of Greek infantry to Persian cavalry, and was one of reasons why Philip of Macedon (and later his son Alexander the Great) decided to wage war on Persia in 334BC.

According to the description which has come down to us from the Athenian historian Xenophon, the equipment of an extra-heavy cavalryman of Cyrus's guard had strong Greek influences: the bronze helmet was decorated with a horsehair plume; there was a scale corselet and bronze scale leg protectors and he was armed with a Greek short sword and iron-tipped javelins. The head of the horse, which could be a Nisaean charger, was protected with a bronze plate, and its breast was covered with a bronze scale apron.

The drawing reconstructs a Persian cavalryman, as described in the text, dressed in the traditional ornate tunic.

PERSIAN EXTRA-HEAVY CAVALRYMAN
fourth century BC

4
Scythian
Horse Archer
fourth century BC

The Scythians were Iranian nomadic tribes who lived in the steppes between the Don and Danube rivers and the Black Sea from the eighth to the second century BC. Before that, they had lived around the Volga river, but were driven from there by the Sarmatians, a related tribe, and moved south-east. During this migration they displaced the native Cimmerians, and came into contact with the Thracians and Celts, as well as with some Greeks. On the territory they conquered they formed their own state, and in the seventh century they crossed the Caucasus range and penetrated the northern parts of Assyria. As its allies they took part in the wars against Egypt, and in 612BC, allied with Babylon and Media, they participated in the destruction of Assyria. Around 512BC, Darius I undertook a great campaign against the Scythians. He conquered Thracia, crossed the Danube on a pontoon bridge, and, according to Herodotus, went as far as the Volga. The Scythians did not put up an organized resistance, but retreated constantly, destroying food and filling in wells behind them, leaving the land devastated. Forced by food shortages, Darius started to retreat, when the Scythians attacked him day and night. Wounded and ill, he was forced to abandon his supply train, and re-cross the Danube into Asia.

Numerous remains of equipment and armament were found in Scythian tombs: composite bows, spears, javelins, axes, swords, daggers and countless bronze and iron scales from which armour was made. Complete horse skeletons with equipment were also found, and armaments were also discovered in women's tombs.

The Scythians were adept at making leather corselets covered with small overlapping scales; each scale set so that it covered half the width of the next scale, in the same way that tiles on a roof overlap. The technique was used to cover leather caps, shields, leg protectors and the aprons on horses' breasts.

Their deadliest weapon was the composite bow, about 80cm/30in long, with a horsehair or animal tendon. This bow was characterized by double action; when an arrow was shot from it, it was driven by both the force of the released tendon and that of the straightening sides of the stave. Taut compression was more important than length of stave, and we know that an arrow shot from such a bow could travel 400 paces. An archer could shoot up to ten arrows a minute, so the force of the fusillade descending on the opponent boggles the mind. The Scythians were skilled riders, and equally good at shooting arrows forwards or backwards.

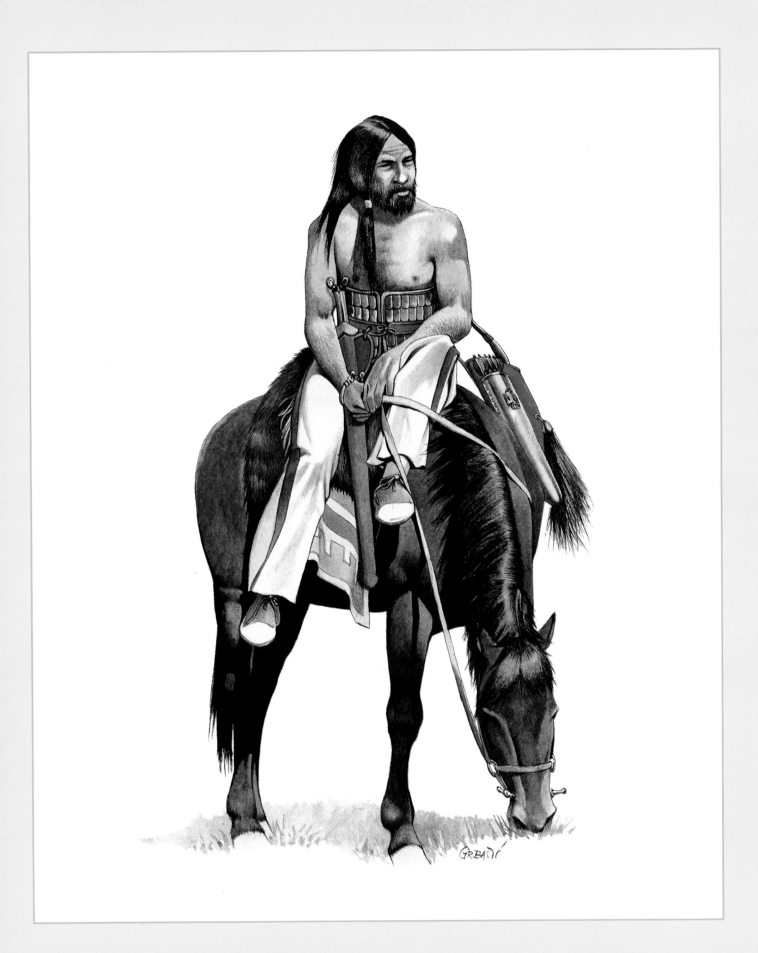

SCYTHIAN HORSE ARCHER
fourth century BC

5
Macedonian Companion (Heteroi) Cavalryman

c. 330BC

All the Macedonian heavy cavalry – 1,800 men in all – was in the senior regiment of the army, its riders recruited from among the sons of the noblest Macedonian families. The regiment consisted of eight squadrons (*ile*), of 200 men each; only the royal one had 400, and these were the *crème de la crème*. A squadron was divided into four smaller units: *tetrarchia*, each with 49 men. Squadrons were commanded by an *ilearch*, and were probably accompanied by a trumpeter.

The figure of 49 was decided very simply: the *tetrarch* was at the head of the unit, with three men in the first line behind him, five in the second, seven in the third and so on up to the last, which had 13 men. This triangular formation was introduced into the Macedonian army by Philip II. It had the advantage of making possible sudden turns to the left or right, at some 45 degrees, which gave the unit more manouverability than the line formation used by the Persian cavalry. There was no need for the whole unit to turn; each man just turned half-left or half-right, and the left or right side of the triangle became the new front line of the unit, with seven Companions (*heteroi*), in the first line and six in the second. The men in the first line were spaced, so those in the second line were not hindered in the charge. This gave the tetrarchia a striking front line of 13 men, and 52 for the whole ile. The four tetrarchias in an ile were arranged like the teeth of a saw, one beside the other, so did not present each other with obstacles to straight or diagonal movement. Several iles made up a cavalry brigade (*hipparchy*) commanded by a *hipparch*. The execution of their complex manoeuvres in battle conditions required strong discipline and a high level of training.

Each squadron of the Companions was recruited from its county and bore its name, and probably had its distinctive colours too. Equipment and weaponry did not differ much from the Greek, but the helmet was distinctly Macedonian. Later, during campaigns lasting several years, lost equipment was made good in various ways, and the appearance of the men became Hellenic. Alexander himself had his helmet damaged by an axe blow from a Persian rider at the Battle of Granicus, and replaced it with a Boeotian helmet.

In ancient times, lions and leopards lived in Macedonia and are mentioned by Roman sources several centuries later. Macedonians and Thracians covered their horses with the skins of these beasts, as we can still see in stone reliefs, which have been preserved.

MACEDONIAN COMPANION (HETEROI) CAVALRYMAN
c. 330 BC

6
Numidian
Light Cavalryman
third century BC

Numidia was a land of shepherds, horsemen and nomads situated in territory now belonging to eastern Algeria and western Tunisia. It was inhabited by tribes later given the name of Berbers, and the most numerous were the Massyli in eastern Numidia and Masaesyli in western Numidia, who each had states headed by kings. From the third century BC, Numidia was dominated by Carthage, which used it as a recruiting ground for light cavalry mercenaries.

In the Second Punic War 218–01BC, the Numidians were initially on the Carthaginian side, but King Sypax of the Masaesyli deposed King Masinissa, who crossed to the Roman side in hopes of regaining his throne, and contributed significantly to their victory. At the Battle of Zama (202BC), 3,000 Numidian cavalry fought for the Carthaginians, while Scipio's army had the assistance of 4,000 cavalry and 6,000 infantry of King Masinissa.

Nearly a century later, when Rome had dealt with its most serious opponents, it was Numidia's turn to be conquered. In the war against King Jugurtha (111–05BC), the Roman army suffered several serious defeats, the worst being at Calma, in 110BC. The Numidians' advantage was the difficult terrain in the interior of their country which hampered the Roman legions, but which their own cavalry handled without problems. However, doggedly taking one stronghold after another, the Romans restricted Jugurtha's space for manoeuvre and finally vanquished him. Numidia ceased to exist.

The Numidian light cavalry distinguished itself in a number of battles. It was particularly effective in reconnaissance, pursuit, ambushes, sudden attacks and tactical deceptions. The men were armed with two or three javelins and light spears, and protected by a small leather shield. They usually had one or two reserve horses, and, according to the Roman writer Livius, switched them in the height of battle by jumping from one to the other in full gallop. They harassed the enemy with continual charges, executed to the accompaniment of terrible shouts and screams, and were often backed up by infantry, also armed with javelins and spears, who covered their retreat.

Roman sources of the third and second century BC describe the Numidians as dark-skinned, dressed in short, sleeveless tunics, and riding stocky, fast, resilient horses without the use of bridles, controlling them with a light rod, or by the use of their voices only.

There is no recorded data on how Numidian mercenaries dressed during the European campaigns, when they would have encountered much colder climates; presumably with blankets or cloaks of animal skins.

NUMIDIAN LIGHT CAVALRYMAN
third century BC

7
Roman
Heavy Cavalryman
first century AD

After the end of the Civil War, the Roman state was consolidated and the army reorganized. Auxiliary units (*auxilia*) became a regular part of the army. In the first century AD, most Roman citizens served as heavy infantry in one of the 25 legions, while cavalry and other auxiliary units were made up of Germans, Gauls and Spaniards. It was mainly for this reason that cavalry was considered an auxiliary force. The cavalry units (*alae*) were named after provinces or towns where they were founded – Ala Noricum, Ala Petriana or Ala Longiniana. Each had its distinctive sign, shown on its standard and on the men's shields. The main standard was carried by the *vexillarius*, while the standard of the *turmae* was carried by the *signifers*. At parades, the *imaginifer* preceded the alae on foot, bearing their symbols, usually in the shape of some animal, and with numerous additional ornaments.

The men of the alae were real combat cavalry, while those of the mixed units (*cohortes equitatae*) could be termed a sort of mounted infantry, whose duties were patrolling, escort, reconnaissance and other general purpose work, rather like the task of the dragoon in later times.

The equipment made for the auxiliary cavalry by Roman armourers was more or less standardized. The most common protective equipment was body-armour – either scale (*lorica squamata*) or mail (*lorica hamata*), with large shoulder pieces. There were also several types of helmets, and it was probably the auxiliary units that popularized various types of helmets, with names such as Gallic or Sassanian, in the Roman army. The man in the drawing has a helmet drawn from the depiction on the tomb (*stela*) of the trooper Dolanus. Units not armed and equipped at the expense of the Roman state kept their own equipment and armaments.

Mounted troops carried either a short Roman sword (*gladius*), or a longer Celtic one (*spatha*), hung on the right side. They were also armed with a light spear (*lancea*), suitable for throwing or thrusting. The horses were rather short (about 145 cm/60 in), like all the others of that time, and simply had a blanket over their backs and a leather saddle without stirrups. The leather harness was often decorated with metal ornaments.

In the Roman army, horses were well taken care of. The writer Oppian has left us a tract, from approximately this period, where he compares horses from all over the huge Roman Empire: North Africa, Egypt, Parthia, Spain and Greece. He concluded that the Spanish horses were the swiftest, while the Moorish ones from Africa were the best for long distances.

ROMAN HEAVY CAVALRYMAN
first century AD

8
Sassanid Cataphract
third century

Although we have little information, we believe that the Aryan tribes, of which the Mitanni and Kassites were two, raised horses. We know that in the last century of their domination the Assyrians had large horses capable of bearing great weights; something that could not be accomplished without planned breeding. However, it was the Medes who left the first written proof of horse breeding. They bred racing horses, whose blood still runs in the veins of today's Arab horses; from the seventh century BC, they started breeding larger horses for heavy cavalry, and these were known as Nisaean chargers. North of the Medes' territory was the state of the Massagetaes, a people of Iranian extraction. It is not known whether they bought horses from the Medes or raised them themselves, but the first mentions of armoured soldiers riding on large armoured horses, dated to the sixth century BC, have been traced to them. Farther north were the related Sarmatians; in the third century BC, making use of their heavy armoured cavalry, they had destroyed the Scythian state. When Media, neighbouring Parthia and more distant Armenia became part of the Persian Empire, the Nisaean charger was used throughout Asia Minor.

With the growing aggressiveness of the role of cavalry, protection of the rider and horse became important. This was specially true of peoples who treated cavalry as the basic arm of the military. One condition had to be fulfilled for equipping a heavy cavalryman: a horse strong enough to carry the weight of its own and the rider's armour. In the third and second centuries BC, the Sarmatians, Armenians and Parthians had such horses and were the first to have fully armoured riders. The Greeks called these warriors the *cataphractii* (covered over). Their equipment was very expensive, and only the aristocracy could afford it: the cataphracts were therefore the elite cavalry of the Parthians and, from the third century AD, the Sassanids. Their principal weapons were a long straight sword and a lance nearly 4 m/13 ft long. The lance was similar to the Greek *sarissa* or the Byzantine *kontos*, and in combat riders held it with both hands. The cataphracts used a dense formation in battle, horse to horse, and attacked at the speed their heavy equipment allowed – a slow trot.

On the banks of the Euphrates, at the Ancient Greek location of Dura Europos (fourth century BC, destroyed by the Sassanids in AD256) a well-preserved set of horse's armour of this period was found. It includes scales for protecting the neck, and larger plates for the animal's head (*chamfrons*). The armour was made of iron scales approximately 6×4.5 cm/2½×2 in and about 4 mm thick. They were rounded at the bottom, had two holes on either side, and four more arranged in a square at the top. The scales were held together by bronze wire threaded through the side holes. A set of armour consisted of about 1,300 scales, arranged as 50 scales in 16 lines on each side of the horse. Armour like this, together with the rest of the horse's equipment, could weigh up to 40 kg/88 lb. There was no armour under the saddle.

SASSANID CATAPHRACT
third century

9
Goth
Heavy Cavalryman
end of fourth century

Three types of horse skeletons were found in excavations at Lake Dümmer in north-west Germany: one was the size of a steppe pony, one medium-sized, and the third belonged to a horse of massive build, probably the Forest or Diluvial horse. These two breeds were the ancestors of modern horses of passive temperament. They lived in northern Europe after the Ice Ages, and were first domesticated about 3,000 years ago in areas later inhabited by the Germans.

In the second century, the Romans followed the mass migration of Goths to the south-east, following the line of the fortified border (*limes*). Descriptions of Goth horsemen and their large horses have come down to us from that time, as well as information about their fighting habits. If a rider chose to dismount and continue the battle on foot, or if he was killed, his horse remained standing in place. For this reason, cavalry attacks were supported by an infantry reserve, whose members were supposed to replace the fallen riders. These foot soldiers held on to the horses' manes and ran alongside – rather dangerous with ponies, as their manes were short, and the men could be trampled under their hooves. With larger and slower horses it was safer, as one could grasp the mane more securely. Stopping the horse after a rider dismounted or was killed was not only a matter of training and discipline but of the animal's docile nature.

The arrival of the Goths on the shores of the Black Sea and their alliances with the Sarmatians and the Alans resulted in pooling of the military experiences of the northern peoples and the ancient Iranian nomadic civilization. The fierce northerners had brought horses about 160 cm/65 in tall. The Sarmatians and the Alans were equally skilled in fighting on horseback and making equestrian equipment and armour. The Sarmatian cataphracts were the heaviest cavalry soldiers of their time, and Rome respected them as formidable opponents, or valued them as allies in auxiliary troops. The Goths acquired a lot of knowledge from them, but not the habit of covering their horses in armour. Goth warriors wore a helmet, and the richer and more important among them a scale or mail corselet. All had wooden shields, and were armed with long Sarmatian swords, a spear and several javelins, which they threw at the enemy. Over time, the Goth cavalry evolved from an auxiliary troop of the infantry into a real fighting force and a decisive factor in battles, moving independently on the battlefield, without reserve riders following on foot.

In AD378, at Adrianople, Alateus and Saphrax, at the head of a force of 20,000 cavalry and 30,000 infantry, mostly Visigoths and some Alans, destroyed the Roman army under Emperor Valens: 10,000 cavalry and 30,000 infantry. First, the Goth cavalry broke the Roman mounted troops and attacked the infantry from the rear. Then the Goth infantry surrounded and routed the enemy.

GOTH HEAVY CAVALRYMAN
end of fourth century

10
Hun Horse Archer
fifth century

The Huns belonged to the Turco-Mongol group of Turanian nomadic peoples, whose ancestral homeland was the Eurasian steppes. For centuries they were a threat to China's northern borders; although the Chinese defeated them often, they did not succeed in subjugating them completely. To protect themselves from the Hun attacks, the Chinese began construction of the Great Wall in 214BC.

Information about the Huns of that period is scarce and mixed with legend. Pushed out of their homeland by other peoples, they erupted on to the historical stage in AD370, when they overran the Alans north of the Black Sea. Then they split, one group heading north to Europe, the other south to Iran.

By the middle of the fifth century, the Huns in Europe were divided into several tribal groups without any central authority. After that, the Hun state gained cohesion and spread to the Rhine after subjugating the Germanic tribes. Attila and his brother Bleda then led their forces over the Danube in AD441, and attacked Byzantium. They massacred defeated opponents, and killed the inhabitants of captured cities, and are now remembered for their cruelty. Fear of the Huns generated incredible stories: that they ate their victims, that they had canine heads.

To protect their country from the Huns, the rulers of the Eastern Roman Empire paid them tribute. In AD451, the Huns invaded the Western Empire, but were defeated on the Catalunian Fields in France. Attila retreated into Hungary with sizeable spoils. He died in AD453 and, according to legend, was buried somewhere near Novi Sad. The Huns, it is said, temporarily diverted the flow of the Tisa, and interred their leader in the river bed.

Roman sources yield curious information about the Huns: that they either sat cross-legged on the ground or rode; they were hardly ever seen walking. They even conducted negotiations with Roman emissaries sitting on horseback. The worst mishap which could befall a Hun warrior in battle was the loss of his horse, as he was quite unaccustomed to fighting on foot. They spent their whole lives in the saddle – fighting, guarding cattle or on the move. Their horses were about 140 cm/55 in tall, short-legged, strong and hardy. They survived the climate – freezing winters and hot summers – of the steppes, and could subsist for days on end with very little food.

The equipment used by ordinary warriors was simple: they had wood-framed saddles or leather pillows, and did not use stirrups or spurs. They controlled their horses with leather reins or whips and their main weapon was the composite bow, which they were adept at using. The manufacture of these bows was complex, consisting of binding several layers of wood with adhesive; this gave them great strength and flexibility. An arrow from this weapon could pierce lamellar armour from a distance of 100 paces.

After conquering the Alans and the Ostrogoths, the Huns adopted some of their customs, as well as some of their equipment, and the nobility apparently used armour and helmets similar to the Goths.

HUN HORSE ARCHER
fifth century

11
Avar
seventh century

The Avars were nomads of Turco-Mongol origin, and were first heard of in Europe in the middle of the fifth century, around the Black and Caspian Seas. After that, nothing is known of them for a whole century; in AD557 they appeared on the Black Sea shores again, and offered Byzantium assistance against other barbarians. Byzantine Emperor Justinian (527–65) paid the Avars to attack the Bulgars, who made frequent incursions into Byzantium. The Don Bulgars were quickly vanquished, and the Avars arrived at the mouth of the Danube, where they subjugated the Slavs. Reinforced with Huns, whom they encountered along the way, and the Bulgarians who had retreated from the Don, the Avars circled the Carpathians and made their way to the Baltic Sea. Around AD567, under the leadership of the founder of the Avar state, Bajan, they settled in the Pannonian valley, and extended their power from the Adriatic shores to Bohemia, and from the Carpathians to the Alps. Although they were numerically inferior, they conquered the many Slav tribes living in these areas, as well as those who came later. The Avars could not have had more than 50,000 warriors, including the Huns and Bulgars who joined them.

Towards the end of the sixth century, the Avars were the strongest military power in Europe. Firmly organized, led by a khan (*kagan*), they retained control of all the conquered areas, concentrating their forces for local supremacy where needed. In the central part of their state, between the Danube and Tisa rivers, they built large camps with defensive earthwork fortifications and palisades, from which they could conduct raids. In battles on open space, the Avars used to place the infantry (consisting of Slavs and other subjugated peoples) in the first ranks, preserving their cavalry for the decisive part of the battle.

Those who came to Europe did not remain nomads like the Huns, but became warrior-horsemen, with a firm military organization and state. They introduced a series of innovations which were soon accepted in Byzantium and other neighbouring states. Among the elements of military equipment copied from the Avars were the wood-framed saddle with leather covering, stirrups, powerful bow, and the use of lamellar armour with neck-protecting gorget which they sometimes wore. Perhaps the most important of these innovations were the stirrups, which made possible advances in the technique of fighting on horseback, thus making cavalry more effective. The rider was more secure in the saddle and controlled the horse easily, giving him more freedom to use his hands, perhaps to carry a larger and heavier shield. The rider could lift himself in the saddle and deliver stronger blows at greater distances than his opponents.

The cornerstone of Avar military power was the armoured cavalry, which fought equally well with bow, spear or lance. As mercenaries in the service of Byzantium, the Avars fitted well into the state's complex organization, which indicates that they excelled in combat tactics which required not only organization but discipline and training.

AVAR
seventh century

12
Carolingian Scola Heavy Cavalryman
ninth century

Charles Martel, a Frank of the Merovingian dynasty, quashed the uprising of the western Franks in Neustria (now Normandy), defeated the Moslems at Poitiers (732) and Berri (737) and, by conquering Aquitaine (now Brittany) enabled his son Pepin the Short to found the Carolingian dynasty in AD751. King Charles I (Charlemagne) (768–814) continued the Frankish expansion initiated by his predecessors. He subjugated the Langobards in Italy, proclaimed himself king of Lombards in 774, vanquished the Avars and spread his rule over the Pannonian valley. After war with the Saxon Germanic tribe, he extended his domain to the Laba river in the north-east. He created a powerful Frankish state which included all the countries of western and central Europe, and proclaimed himself Roman Emperor in 800.

By the time of Charlemagne, the feudal system had taken deep root in the Frankish state. His laws (*capitularia*) regulated obligatory military service and the recruiting system. At his call the feudal lords gathered at a predetermined point; failure to turn up resulted in a fine and confiscation of holdings. Every rider had to have body-armour (*brunia*), shield, spear, helmet, sword and knife, a fully equipped horse, a wagon with all the necessary tools (axe, spade, pickaxe, auger) and provisions for three months.

It is now impossible to determine whether brunia was a particular type of armour, named after the metal platelets and rings (*brynja*) sewn on to a goatskin shirt, or just a generic term for body-armour. Carolingian knights used armour found throughout Europe, of the type worn by Avars and Byzantines: lamellar, mail or scale hauberk and mail coif. The sword was the most expensive and important piece of equipment; its production required great forging skill, and its quality reflected the status of its owner. Although their first neighbours – Arabs, Lombards and Avars – used stirrups, the Carolingians showed little interest at first in this particular piece of equipment, as their battle tactics gave equal importance to fighting on horseback and on foot. Stirrups became standard equipment only towards the end of the ninth century.

Charlemagne also had a standing force organized into independent units (*scarae*), numbering several hundred men, under the local administration and command of a count (*graf*). These units guarded the borders of the state and garrisoned important forts; they could also be used for police duty. Several border counties were joined in administrative provinces called *marcae*, under the rule of a *comes marcae*, or *markgraf*.

From the time of King Pepin, the sovereign was protected by a standing elite unit of noblemen (*scola*), who lived at court, or in the near vicinity. It was expected that a nobleman's military role would benefit from the profits of his estate, so the richer warriors had to have better equipment and use it more effectively. The scola were the elite and best mounted and equipped fighting unit of the Carolingian cavalry.

CAROLINGIAN SCOLA HEAVY CAVALRYMAN
ninth century

13
Byzantine Klibanophoros
tenth century

In the tenth and eleventh centuries, the period of their greatest power, the Byzantine horsemen were the best paid and best equipped and organized military force of their time.

During the rule of Emperor Nicephoros II (963–9), Byzantium, free from the Bulgar threat, undertook military enterprises in Asia Minor. Cyprus and Syria were conquered, and the Arabs taken on in Palestine. The state treasury grew richer. Nicephoros formed units modelled on the late Roman heavy cavalry (*clibanarii*) and the extra-heavy (*klibanophoroi*). This name derived from the *klibanion*, a corselet used by the Byzantine riders; its name in turn came from the Latin *clibanarius* (heavily armoured horseman). Because their equipment was very expensive, the klibanophoroi probably only existed in the guard (*tagmata*).

On the battlefield, the klibanophoroi used a wedge formation, with 20 men in the first line, 24 in the second, and four more in each following line. The last, twelfth, line had 64 men, and the whole unit 504. A formation more frequently used had 10 lines and 384 men. Approximately every fourth and fifth man was armed with a bow instead of a lance, and positioned slightly to the rear inside the wedge. There were probably three units of klibanophoroi in the tagmata, totalling between 1,000 and 1,500 men. Every unit bore its own pennant on lances, and had vestments of a distinctive colour.

The klibanophoroi were armed with a lance (*kontos*), about 4 m/13 ft long, which had been adopted from the Sarmatians and Alans, and a sword (*spathion*, from the Latin *spatha*) with a 90 cm/35 in blade. The first four ranks of klibanophoroi also carried several short darts (*marzabarboulon*) in a leather case hanging from the saddle. Byzantine cavalry used three basic types of protection: mail, scale and lamellar armour, the last being the most often used. The lamellae were mostly of iron, although leather and horn were used too. Riders also wore a wide-skirted, knee-length topcoat with short sleeves (*epilorikion*), made of padded and quilted cotton, leather and felt, at least 2 cm/1 in thick and worn over the corselet. The lower parts of the legs were protected by iron graves (*podopsella*), and the forearms with splint armour vambraces (*chiropsella*). Horse-armour was made of horn or iron lamellae or mail, but multi-layered felt covering is also mentioned. Headgear was of the same materials, and metal chamfrons were possibly used as well.

After defeat at the hands of the Saljuqs at Manzikert, in 1071, the klibanophoroi ceased to exist.

BYZANTINE KLIBANOPHOROS
tenth century

14
Arab (Andalusian) Light Horseman
tenth century

Arabia, a peninsula of south-west Asia, is nearly 2,300 km/1,500 miles long and about 2,000 km/1,250 miles wide. In its centre is an arid plateau, bordered by the Great Nufud Desert to the north and the even larger Al-Rab Al-Hali Desert on the south. There is some arable land along the shore and in isolated oases on the plateau, but there are no permanent rivers, and average summer temperatures range from −6°C at night to +45°C in the daytime.

Geographically uninteresting, Arabia was for a long time on the sidelines of history. The great changes taking place in Asia – the wars of the Assyrians, Babylonians, Egyptians, Persians, Macedonians and Romans – affected only the north. The peoples inhabiting Arabia, given the blanket term Arabs, undertook only occasional military and pillaging raids outside their domain, and quickly returned. They rode camels, and were nomadic warriors, products of the endless deserts of this giant peninsula.

Ancient sources make no mention of their having horses. The Old Testament speaks only of camels and asses, as do Assyrian and Persian records. In AD622, Muhammad attacked a rich caravan with 1,000 camels on the way from Gaza to Mecca. His army consisted of 314 men, 72 camels and only two horses. The armed forces of the richest and most powerful Arab town of the period, Mecca, had 750 camels and only 100 horses.

Horses probably came to Arabia through Syria and Yemen, which had long been in Persian hands. In 639, when the Arabs invaded Egypt, their forces are said to have included 3,000 Yemenite horsemen, which is the first mention of a significant cavalry force on the peninsula.

During the sixth and seventh centuries, several factors came together in this area which resulted in an outstanding breed, impossible to confuse with any other: the Arabian horse, considered the purest of all. Geographical, climatic and economic conditions in the desert expanses of Arabia combined to produce a horse with a strong constitution, great resilience and modest demands for food and water; evidently an animal with vast military potential. The nomad-warrior inhabitants of the desert relied solely on horses and slow camels for transport. They had to cover great distances without much food or water, so for centuries they bred their animals selectively to reinforce the characteristics they needed. Dependence on horses resulted in the Arabs developing a great love for them, so much attention was devoted to their appearance. Long selective breeding, sometimes of closely related animals, in conditions which did not change for a thousand years, gave the Arabian horse morphological and physiological characteristics so stable that their inheritance is certain.

The illustration shows an Arab light horseman of the type seen in Moslem-ruled Andalusia, in Spain, in the tenth century.

ARAB (ANDALUSIAN) LIGHT HORSEMAN
tenth century

15
Norman Knight
eleventh century

The Normans (derived from Northman) were northern Germanic tribes inhabiting the Scandinavian peninsula and Denmark. They were isolated from the other Germanic tribes, and developed without much outside influence. Conditions of life were difficult because of the barren ground, and these tribes had turned early to the sea; able sailors, they raided the coasts and islands of the North Sea and Atlantic countries. In the ninth century, they left their homeland en masse and moved towards Europe in search of a better existence.

The Frankish state could not stand up to the incursion of several large groups of Normans along the Seine valley into central France. In 911, King Charles III ('the Simple') ceded them land which was named Normandie after its new inhabitants. There they found feudalism, and, with their inborn sense of organization, they developed an economic basis sufficient to support a powerful military caste (*milites*). Although similar processes were going on throughout Europe, the Normans paid most attention to knighthood and chivalry.

Norman raiders gave a new dimension to mounted warfare, which became deadlier than ever before, and during the next four centuries, infantry could not deal with the Norman attacks. The secret was in the sheer strength of their attack with lances. Three elements contributed to this: a high wooden saddle with a protective pommel, fastened with two leather straps, one crossing the horse's chest, the other its belly; the rider's straight-legged position; and gripping the lance (when used) tightly between the chest and upper arm. Never before had saddle been fastened to horse so firmly, rider planted in the saddle so securely, and lance gripped so tightly; never before had the impact of fully equipped rider and horse been transmitted so strongly. Equally, a rider thus firmly anchored could withstand a stronger lance blow without being unseated.

However, there were drawbacks to this arrangement. The deeply ensconced rider, with legs outstretched, had only limited lateral mobility, and was more vulnerable to attack from the sides and back; also, he could not stand in the saddle to deliver strong and far-reaching sword strikes. These shortcomings had to be compensated for in other ways: primarily by better rider protection and increased control of the horse.

The mail hauberk grew in size (it now weighed up to 15 kg/33 lb), reaching the knees, and full-length sleeves were added. The rider's left side was protected with a kite-shaped shield, which was held in the hand, but, because of its great weight, the shield strap was slung over the right shoulder.

In this era of knights, there was increasing dependence on their horses, and their choice, breeding and training gained steadily in importance.

NORMAN KNIGHT
eleventh century

16
Knight
twelfth century

In twelfth century England, France and Germany, the profile of members of the caste of mounted warriors was clearly defined. The close connection between knights and their mounts is apparent in the words for them in various languages: from the French *cheval* (horse), we have *chevalier*, *cavaliere* (Italian), and *caballero* (Spanish); the German word for knight *ritter* (rider) was the basis for the Polish *rycer*. Only in English was the etymology different; knight comes from the Anglo-Saxon *cniht*, meaning household retainer or servant.

In the life of a knight, the horse occupied a position of great importance, and was, literally, his right-hand companion. Horses were led by knights or their squires on their right-hand sides, and this was the origin of the term destrier for war-horse.

The medieval knight occupied a precisely defined position in society; his relationship with his superiors and inferiors was codified. He was primarily a warrior, and his rank, authority and obligations derived from this fact. He owed certain duties and obligations to his feudal liege (although free from feudal taxes), and certain obligations and duties were due to him from his serfs. His position and wealth depended on the size of his fiefdom, but a significant source of his income was war booty.

In the beginning, knighthood could be conferred by another knight, but as the feudal system developed this turned into a privilege of the sovereign, and became linked with religious ritual. This hierarchy of authority was important to a ruler, because without his knights he was powerless to enforce his will.

The norms for behaviour among knights were set down in a code of chivalry, but this did not govern their behaviour towards other classes, except for biblical injunctions of mercy to the weak and charity to the poor.

Induction into the knighthood was a special ceremony. The ancestry and military prowess of the candidates were important, and it was rare indeed for an outstanding warrior not of noble birth to become a knight. The sons of knights and noblemen began serving as pages at court or with another knight at the age of seven. At 14 they became squires, and at 21 they were proposed for induction into the knighthood.

KNIGHT
twelfth century

17
Saljuq (Turcoman)
thirteenth century

The early history of the Turks is lost in legend. They are first mentioned in Chinese sources in the fourteenth century BC. In the second century BC they are the warrior tribes Hiung-nu or Hsiung-nu. The name Turks first appears in the sixth century AD, in the Chinese form of Tu-küe, which Greek sources render as Turqos.

Turkish tribes headed westwards, and arrived in Asia Minor in the ninth century, where they came into contact with the Arabians, and accepted Islam. For a time they served as mercenaries of the caliph of Baghdad. In the tenth century, under the rule of Seljuk ben Dukak (Tukak), they formed a union with the Oghuz group of tribes, and adopted the name Seljuk or Saljuq. Dukak's successor, Tughril Beg, took advantage of Persia's weakness and conquered Khorasan, Azerbaijan, Media and Iran. In 1055 he captured Baghdad, and proclaimed himself King of East and West as Amir al-Umara. He founded the Saljuq dynasty which would rule from the Bosphorus to Turkestan for the next 100 years. His successors, Alp Arslan Muhammad ibn Dawud (1063–72) defeated the Byzantine army at Manzikert in 1071 and continued the drive westwards. Malikshah (1071–92) extended his rule over Syria, Georgia and most of Asia Minor. The Saljuq state was then at the height of its power. After the death of Malikshah, members of the Saljuq dynasty divided the state into Rum (Anatolia) and the Baghdad Caliphate.

The appearance of the Saljuqs and their mass settlement in the Middle East and Asia Minor caused a series of socio-economic and ethnic changes in the area in the eleventh and twelfth centuries. Their capture of Jerusalem in 1076 was one of the causes of the Crusades. Although defeated in the First Crusade, the Saljuqs of Rum subsequently blocked the overland route to Jerusalem, and were in constant conflict with the Crusaders.

In their ancestral homeland, in Central Asia, the Turks had subjugated related nomadic tribes – the Turcomans – and forced them to join the move to the west, but they remained politically unreliable. To keep them occupied and prevent their meddling in internal matters, the Saljuqs tried to keep them engaged in wars and settled them in border areas. The Turcoman warriors at the borders were called *ghazis*, a name later used for all defenders of the Moslem world.

The bulk of the Saljuq forces facing the Crusaders at the borders consisted of Turcomans. They were excellent riders, and were armed with deadly bows. They used hit-and-run nomad tactics, firing their arrows from about 50 metres/55 ft; even at that distance, they could pierce mail coif. Their equipment was made according to the Asiatic tradition, and richly ornamented in the Arab style.

SALJUQ (TURCOMAN)
thirteenth century

18
Knight Hospitaller
thirteenth century

The name 'Crusades' is used for a series of military expeditions organized by the Christian states of central and western Europe against the Muslims of the Middle East from the eleventh to the thirteenth centuries, and the struggle to preserve and expand the territories conquered. The immediate cause of the Crusades was the expansion of the Saljuq Turks into the Middle East and Asia Minor. In 1095, at Piacenza, Byzantine representatives addressed the Church Council, explaining the danger from the Saljuq Turks. Their capture of Jerusalem made pilgrimages, which had gone on undisturbed for centuries, much more difficult. At the Council in Clermont, in 1095, Pope Urban II called on the faithful to liberate the tomb of Christ in Jerusalem.

At first, Orders of Knights were founded with the funding and assistance of the Catholic church. They started out as charities, but after the reorganization of 1118–20 became military institutions. Members of the military Orders were divided into knights, priests and serving brethren, and each Order was headed by a grand master, directly subordinated to the pontiff.

The best-known Orders were the Templars and Hospitallers, founded in Jerusalem, and the Teutonic Knights, founded in Palestine, but there were numerous lesser ones: Calatrava, Santiago, Alcantra, St George of Alfama, San Stefano of Tuscany, Brethren of the Sword, and so on.

The Order of Red Knights of St John of Jerusalem was founded in 1070 as a charitable institution: Hospice of St John the Almoner of Jerusalem, with the aim of treating the wounded and ill soldiers and pilgrims, hence the name Hospitallers. Baldwin of Boulogne, third ruler of Jerusalem, supported the hospital; after vanquishing an Egyptian force, he endowed it with one tenth of the booty, setting an example which was followed for a long time. The funds which the Order acquired were sufficient to set up a chain of hospitals in the Holy Land.

In 1113, the Hospitallers were established as an independent religious order by papal bull. According to their charter, members were free to fight, if necessary, to protect their hospitals. In 1130, another papal order decreed a white cross on a red background as their flag, and the white cross on their black mantles became their symbol. In 1248, the mantle was replaced by a more practical black coat with the cross on the front.

In 1142, the Order had eight castles, the best-known of which was Krak des Chevaliers, with a crew of 200 knights and sergeants. The Hospitallers and Templars were the best fighting force in the Holy Land in this period, and were always placed in the position of honour in the battle order – the right wing.

KNIGHT HOSPITALLER
thirteenth century

19
Mameluke
Armoured
Cavalryman
thirteenth century

The last Egyptian caliph of the Fatimid dynasty died in 1171. The new ruler, Salah al-Din Yusuf ibn Ayyub (1169–93), better known in Europe as Saladin, the founder of the Ayyubid dynasty, based his military power on the Mameluke. A Mameluke (Arabic, *mamalik*, Turkish, *ghulam*) was a slave or prisoner offered freedom in exchange for military service, or a captured boy raised in a special military school and converted to Islam.

Unable to expand their army from domestic resources, the Ayyubids were forced to rely on the Mamelukes. They bought Kurds and Syrians, and took into their service hordes of Turkish ghulams and Turcomans who, fleeing from the Mongols, appeared in the Levant at this time. Mamelukes established themselves as the basis of Egypt's military strength during the rule of Sultan Salah Nagm al Din (1240–9), who devoted special attention to recruiting young Cherkezis from the Caucasus. They were subjected to rigorous training, especially in archery, and then inducted into the Egyptian army, usually into the guard. About 10,000 Mamelukes, well armed and well mounted, comprised the nucleus of the Egyptian forces. The remaining mass, made up of Bedouin horsemen and recruits, was of little value, and served only as support for the Mamelukes, who chose their officers themselves. They were awarded land according to rank, and having demonstrated their superior fighting skills in wars against the Crusaders and the Mongols, they gained more privileges, influence and independence. Increasingly they participated in the government of the country, and finally succeeded in gaining the throne of Egypt.

The first Mameluke sultan of the throne of Egypt was Aibey (1250–7). He initiated the era of the Bahri Mamelukes (of Turkish and Armenian origin), whose rule lasted until 1390. They provided 24 sultans, the most important of whom was Baybars al Malik al Zahir al Din al Bundugari (1260–77), successful in organization, war and politics, and the real creator of Mameluke power. He extended the borders of Egypt, stopped the Mongols at Ain Jalut in 1260, captured the forts of Jaffa and Antioch and crushed the might of the Crusaders. The sultan with the longest reign, Al Nasir (1293–1340), was thrice outnumbered and defeated by the Mongols at Homs in 1299, but was victorious east of Damascus in 1303.

The Burgi Mamelukes (of Cherkezi origin), named after a Cairo fort they garrisoned, succeeded the Bahri, and provided 23 sultans. Militarily, their most successful sultan was Kaitbey (1468–95), who defeated two Turkish Ottoman armies in Anatolia, and prevented a Turkish landing on the Egyptian coast. In 1490 he again defeated them at Caesarea (Mazaca-Kayseri). However, the Turks decisively defeated the Mamelukes at Ridaniya, near Cairo, in 1517, and conquered Egypt.

MAMELUKE ARMOURED CAVALRYMAN
thirteenth century

20
Mongol Warrior
thirteenth century

Nomadic life in the vast steppes of Asia made excellent warriors of the Mongols: conditions of life were difficult, and enemies and armed robbers abounded, threatening their cattle and families. The Mongols were natural riders, good shots from horseback and on foot, resilient, had small needs, and were skilled in warfare and combat. They had a quality then unknown in the west: team spirit.

During the lean winter months, hunts were organized to feed the family and the tribe. These horseback forays, in which bows were used, foreshadowed in many ways their future military campaigns. The leader of the hunt had to be obeyed, and complete cooperation was expected of all participants. The trail was followed in absolute silence, the hunters communicating by visual signals, and this could go on for days. Once the quarry was tracked down, the hunters surrounded it, and shot it with arrows or captured it with lassoes. If a hunter allowed an animal to escape from the circle, he was severely punished.

Building on the basis of these small hunting bands, Temujin organized one 'large hunting band' – the army. It consisted of over 100,000 men, and ensnared many opposing forces in its trap during the Mongol conquests of 1211–80. Discipline was strict, as evidenced by preserved fragments of Gengis Khan's law, the *Jasa*. Special attention was devoted to matters of heredity, obedience and treason, but even without these strictures, obedience and respect for superiors seems to have been an inbred trait of the Asian nomadic tribes.

All men between the ages of 15 and 60 had to go to war. Nobody was paid, but everyone had an equal share of the spoils of war; part being reserved for the great khan. Every warrior carried his own tools, food bowl, supplies, and waterproof bag for crossing rivers; each man had three to five horses, which could be used as food if the need arose. The horses were about 14 hands tall, and were related to the wild horse discovered in the last century by Colonel Przevalsky in the steppes of what is now Mongolia. The Mongols usually rode mares, because of the milk, and because these were followed at a distance by foals and stallions, who helped to keep the herd of reserve horses together.

The best warriors were taken into the khan's guard (*keshik*), which numbered 2,000 men until 1206, and 10,000 thereafter. It was divided into the day watch (*turghaut*), 1,000 strong, the night watch (*kabtaut*), also of 1,000 men, the sharpshooters (*korchin*) (1,000) and the khan's personal guards (*baatut*), numbering 7,000. The guard remained under arms even in peacetime, and assured the khan's rule. Even though it was mostly made up of the aristocracy, others could reach high positions in the army according to their merit and regardless of origin.

MONGOL WARRIOR
thirteenth century

21
Russian Druzynik
thirteenth century

In the thirteenth century, the Mongols captured vast expanses of north-eastern Russia, and Russian principalities which did not enter directly into the new Mongol state, known as the Golden Horde, became its vassals. They were allowed to keep their social systems, but were supervised by a special military and administrative organization set up by the Mongols. The weakened Russian states in the north were attacked by the Swedes, Teutons and Lithuanians, but the Novgorod and Pskov principalities resisted these onslaughts.

In the eleventh and twelfth centuries, Russia consisted of a number of independent principalities with economic and feudal relationships different from those in the west. Until the Mongol invasion, a military-feudal nobility existed, and was organized in over 100 *druzhinas*. The druzhina, which retained the name formerly used by a chieftain's bodyguard, was a prince's retinue of personal warriors. Members, called *druzyniks*, were granted estates (*pomestiia*) in exchange for their services. Once granted, ownership of these estates was free of all obligations, and if a druzynik decided to switch allegiances, he took his land with him to the new prince's state. The estates were thus allodial, not feudal.

The druzhina was divided into senior and junior members, the senior members being *boyars* (great nobles) and state officers. The juniors made up the grid, and could be promoted upon coming of age, or by acquiring sufficient retainers to serve the prince in their own right. By the twelfth century, however, the boyars had become very powerful, and their personal appearances in the druzhina became rather infrequent; princes had to rely on the grid.

Militarily, the druzhina was organized according to the decade system: *desiatniia* (10 men), *sotnia* (100) and *tisiach* (1,000). The Kiev, Novgorod and, later, Moscow principalities had the largest druzhinas.

The Russian principalities waged practically continuous warfare against a series of Asiatic nomadic tribes, among them the Pechenegs, Cumans, Uzes, and the Mongol conquest in 1240 was the culmination of these protracted hostilities. These prolonged contacts ensured that Russia would, in military matters, gravitate towards the east, and not towards Europe, and the equipment worn by Russian warriors illustrates this. Another feature was the nobles' conservatism: thirteenth century-style equipment was still in widespread use in the sixteenth century: scale armour with or without coif, lamellar or leather corselets with stitched-on rings and long mail corselets.

The pictured horseman is wearing a Byzantine-type *kapalin* helmet, and Asiatic plate vambraces.

RUSSIAN DRUZYNIK
thirteenth century

22
French Knight
1370

Over a period of one thousand years, the development of protective equipment for warriors advanced very slowly. It consisted mostly of mail, scale and lamellar armour, and the period between changes was measured in hundreds of years. However, from the second half of the fourteenth century, the period of plate armour began, and changes appeared every 20 to 30 years. The need for improvement was dictated by the increasing deadliness of weapons, especially the couched lance and the infantry crossbow. In 1139, the church prohibited the use of the crossbow in combat against Christians.

Records exist which show that some metal plates were used for knights' protection, for example, the description of the fight between Richard, Count of Poitou (later Richard I of England), and William de Barres, in which each combatant wore a plate of worked iron beneath the hauberk and *aketon* (end of twelfth century). At this time, too, body defence of plate armour (*cuire*) is first explicitly mentioned; this was almost certainly synonymous with *cuirass* or *curace*. After 1250, the development of plate armour was a general process and many tomb decorations from the end of the thirteenth and beginning of the fourteenth centuries depict plates for leg (*gauntlets*), throat (*gorgets*) and arm (*vambraces*) protection. However, it is much more difficult to fix the date of appearance of body-armour (coat of plates or *côte à plates*), as it was habitually worn between the hauberk and surcoat. It is rarely seen in illustrations before the third decade of the fourteenth century, when the front of the surcoat was shortened. Excavation of the mass grave of the Gotland warriors, buried after the Battle of Wisby (1361) was enlightening. Reconstruction has shown that a coat enveloping the body consisted of 22 separate plates joined by rivets. The plates were covered with cloth, on both the outside and the inside.

The second half of the fourteenth century saw the increasing use of the *bascinet* or *honskull* helmet with a movable visor (German, *klappvisier*). There is a theory that the modern military salute, with the right hand raised to the cap's edge, derives from the movement the knight made to lift his visor when addressed by a superior. This century saw further improvements in the protective equipment of the French knights – at the time the best in Europe – but it also saw the end of nearly 400 years of domination by feudal forces of cavalry over infantry on the battlefields of France. The French knights were defeated by the Flemish infantry at the Battle of Curtrai (1302), and by the English at Crecy (1346) and at Poitiers (1356). The English victories were predominantly due to archers armed with Welsh longbows, an arrow from which could kill a knight's horse at some distance, and at 20–30 paces could pierce his plate armour. The French learned nothing from these battles; their tactics remained the same, and the race for armour improvement continued.

FRENCH KNIGHT
1370

23
Destrier
fourteenth century

In AD476, the Germans toppled the Western Roman Empire, and their leader, Odoacer, proclaimed himself king. In 488, their state was subjugated by the Ostrogoths, whose rule was not long-lived either: Byzantium soon acquired control of Italy. Finally, in 568, the northern part of the Apennine peninsula was conquered by the Langobards (Lombards), one of the Germanic tribes, and Italy was divided into two parts: Langobardia, in the north with its seat at Pavia, and Romagna in the south, ruled by Byzantium.

In the third century, the Goths had brought the first heavy horses to the south-east of Europe; three centuries later, the related Langobards imported similar horses to northern Italy. In the Po river valley, they found favourable conditions for raising horses: fertile ground, a subject people who knew how to work it, and other remains of the most developed civilization in Europe. In the eighth century, with the help of Byzantium, the Franks conquered the Langobards, the best horsemen in central Europe, and assimilated them into their army.

In the age of the knights, the most popular horses for heavy cavalry were raised in northern Italy. The most expensive horses, those used for court ceremony and prestige, parades and hunts, were bought in Spain. The blood of the north Italian and Spanish breeds flows nowadays in the veins of many modern horses.

The name destrier was derived from the Latin *dextrarius* (in the right hand). It was a very tall horse, 17 hands on average, heavy and strong. It was rather slow, though, and had little acceleration; it was not therefore used in combat but only for jousting. The horse mostly used by knights in battle was the courser, which was smaller, lighter and cheaper. In the twelfth century, a knight usually had two horses, but this rose to three or four late in the following century.

Another type of horse used in combat was the rounsey, akin to the courser but without special breeding. It cost comparatively little and was used by sergeants and horsemen without the rank of knight.

Besides heavy horses, other breeds in use in England in the fourteenth century were the Irish hobby and the Scottish pony known as galloway or hackney, both about 12–14 hands. Horses of no particular breed, but occasionally used by knights, were called palfreys.

DESTRIER
fourteenth century

24
Sergeant
fourteenth century

Sergeant (from the Latin *servientes*) was a term with many different meanings. In feudal terminology, he was usually a vassal without knightly status. His fee, smaller than a knight's, was called a serganty (*serianteria*, *seriantia*), and the services he offered were mostly military, but sometimes domestic or agricultural. It seems likely that a knight's retainers also bore the name of sergeants, although the terms *satellites* and *clientes* were also applied to them. Finally, the term is also used by modern historians to describe all non-knightly soldiers of the period, infantry or cavalry, feudal or not.

By the twelfth century, sergeants usually fought on horseback. Their equipment seems to have been similar to the knights', but lighter. Some evidence suggests that it was even lighter than is usually thought; late eleventh- and early twelfth-century manuscripts often show knights followed by men equipped only with helmet, shield, sword and lance, who are undoubtedly sergeants. Numerous documents show that the service of two mounted sergeants was considered equal to that of one knight, but the number of knights decreased in time, and non-knightly combatants increased, so that the terms *milites* and *servientes*, defined in the earlier centuries, began to be blurred. During the thirteenth century, the term man-at-arms was used increasingly, and applied to all armoured horsemen regardless of status.

After the rise of heraldry, sergeants sometimes carried their lord's device or badge on the shield, pennon or surcoat. Some of the most important noblemen could equip up to several hundred sergeants in their retinues with liveries in their colours.

Available data suggest that the number of sergeants was usually roughly equal to the number of knights, but sometimes as much as double. Philip Augustus of France could usually raise 257 knights and 267 sergeants; for the campaign of 1214 (Bouvines) he called on 2,000 knights and 5,000 sergeants. At the Battle of Muret (1213), Simon de Montfort had 270 knights and 500 sergeants; in 1264, Henry III of England hired 500 knights and 1,000 sergeants, and at Crecy (1346), Edward III led 1,200 knights and 1,743 sergeants.

In the order of battle, mounted sergeants were usually mixed with the knights. It was not uncommon, though, to find them forming the whole front rank, presumably to soften up the enemy before the knights' charge. This had to be decisive, as it could usually be launched only once. For example, sergeants formed the first line of the French army at Bouvines and at Benevento in 1266.

SERGEANT
fourteenth century

25
Mercenary in Service of Condottieri
mid-fifteenth century

The *condottieri* were leaders of Italian mercenary companies (*compagnie di ventura*) from the fourteenth to the sixteenth century. The term is derived from *condotta*, the temporary contract by which the company entered the service of a state, city or dukedom. The *banco di condotta* was the name for the exact register of soldiers, retainers and horses of a mercenary company, used for accounting with employers.

The condottieri, unlike other mercenary leaders, were absolute masters of their companies, and gathered their soldiers for their own interests, profit, power and glory. The first in Italy were foreigners: the German knight von Urslingen, the Provençal Franciscan Fra Moriale, the former London tailor Sir Hawkwood. The era of the condottieri was opened by the victory at Mariano (1380) of Alberico da Barbiano, in service of the pope, over Gascoigne and Breton mercenaries.

They were often feudal lords, like Barbiano, Malatesta, Borgia, F. Colonna and P. Colonna, and in such cases the nucleus of their forces consisted of their serfs. However, some were plebeians – outstanding warriors like Sforza and Carmagnola, who gathered professional soldiers eager to profit from their reputations. In either case, the condottieri chose, trained, disciplined and paid their soldiers, the contracts being between them and the employers. They were exclusively responsible for the actions of their men, and had unlimited power over them, but also the responsibility of looking after them. Contracts usually defined the term of service, the pay and the strength of the company. For example, in 1448 an eighth-month contract was made between the Duke of Milan and the Marquis of Monferrato, calling for a force of 700 lances and 500 infantry, and providing for a sum of 6,000 forints a month. The marquis was also given 40 gold coins for the equipment (*prestanza*) of each of the lances. Unlike earlier foreign mercenary companies which had ravaged Italy, the condottieri, who were closely tied to some areas, had no interest in destroying the population physically or economically.

At this time Milan was the largest European centre of armour production. The characteristic product of the city's workshops was called the Italian Armour, or Lombard- or Milan-style. Most of the sets worn by the soldiers of the condottieri and sold throughout Europe bore the identification marks of the Missaglia family, which owned most of the armoury workshops in Milan in the fifteenth century. The first manufactured homogeneous (or full) set of cavalry armour, now housed in Chuburg, was made in one of these in 1420, owned by the Matsch family of Milan. A few years later, a similar set was made in Landshut, in Germany, the most important rival centre. By the mid-fifteenth century, full armour had spread throughout Europe.

MERCENARY IN SERVICE OF CONDOTTIERI
mid-fifteenth century

26
Burgundian
Mounted
Archer

c. 1475

Towards the end of the Middle Ages, the feudal armed forces of the Duchy of Burgundy became less powerful. In 1472, for example, only 2,524 horsemen were recruited, together with 807 other nobles not wealthy enough to have their own horses. In vain Charles the Bold (1467–77) tried in a series of detailed orders to define the duties of his feudal subjects; finally, he was forced to follow the example of France and create Compagnies d'Ordonnance, troops always at hand. The first of these were formed in 1471. An order of 1472 envisaged 1,200 men-at-arms, 3,000 mounted archers, 600 mounted crossbowmen, 1,000 archers on foot, 2,000 pikemen and 600 handgunners, a total of 8,400 men. However, these levels were never achieved for lack of funds. Their final formation was decided by the Great Order of 1473, the most important of fifteenth-century documents dealing with military organization. It offers a wealth of detail, and also touches on questions of tactics.

The smallest basic unit was called the *lance*. Its mounted members were one man-at-arms, one swordsman (*coustillier*), one valet and three archers; dismounted were one crossbowman, one pikeman and one handgunner – nine men in all. Six lances made up a *chambre*, four chambres a squadron, and four squadrons a company. A full company had 900 men, 600 of them mounted.

The equipment of some of the members of a lance was fixed: a man-at-arms had to have full armour, three horses (one each for the page and swordsman), a war saddle and a horse's helmet (*chanfron*); moreover, the saddle and helmet had to be decorated with blue and white plumes. He also had to display a vermilion cross of St Andrew on his armour. The mounted archers had to have 30 arrows each, plus a bow, a two-handed sword and a dagger. Archers usually wore blue-and-white jackets with red St Andrew's crosses.

Just before the serious defeat at Morat, the duke's mounted arm consisted of 1,741 men-at-arms and 4,062 mounted archers (1,377 of them English).

The Great Order also defined the salaries of the men, which were paid every three months: a man-at-arms was paid 15 francs for himself and his two retainers, who were not counted as combatants; a mounted archer was paid five francs, the handgunners and crossbowmen four francs and the pikemen two patars.

The mounted archers of Burgundy distinguished themselves in several battles, including their last – at Nancy, in 1477, where many died along with Charles the Bold.

BURGUNDIAN MOUNTED ARCHER
c. 1475

27
Knight in
'Gothic' Armour
end of fifteenth century

The gothic was the second important period in the development of European medieval art. The name originated during the Renaissance, and had a pejorative ring: the Goths were barbarians.

Until the middle of the fifteenth century, the largest centre for the manufacture of armour was Milan, and Italian armour was foremost in quality and beauty. However, from then on, European feudal lords increasingly bought armour and swords from the south German towns of Mühlau, Augsburg and Landshut. German armour had an appearance distinctly different from the Italian, but achieved the same level of quality. As armour manufacture in Milan was connected with the Missaglia family, so in Augsburg the foremost shop was that of the Helmschmeids. Lorenz Helmschmeid (1445–1516) was one of the greatest armourers of the century.

Unlike Italian armour, which had smooth rounded plates, German armour was covered with fluting, which recalled the broken arches of gothic architecture and, besides being decorative, reinforced the plates. One of the greatest advantages of 'gothic' armour was that it was adapted to the human anatomy, offering maximum protection with minimum weight and limitation of movement.

For example, a long mail shirt (hauberk) weighed about 15 kg/33 lb, and a knight had to bear this whole weight on his shoulders. A whole 'gothic' suit of armour was never more than 25 kg/55 lb in weight, and its plates were fastened to the corresponding body parts from the inside by leather straps, so that the weight was more evenly distributed and the armour more comfortable to wear. The insides of the shoulder and arm joints were not covered by plates so as to permit maximum mobility; they were protected by mail. But this was also its greatest weakness, as it could be pierced at these points with swords or daggers. Another drawback was that, for easier movement, the helmet was not fastened to the shoulders, as with later models. Thus, hard blows with clubs, swords or other weapons which were not sufficient to pierce the helmet were still enough to put the warrior out of combat, as the force of these blows was absorbed not by the shoulders but by the head. Because of these deficiencies, gothic armour was replaced in the sixteenth century by heavier and more compact types. In the last third of the fifteenth century, horse-armour was produced in Germany too, also in the gothic style. A suit produced in Landshut in 1480 weighed 31 kg/68 lb without the saddle.

The earliest preserved suit of horse-armour (bard), bearing the mark of a Milanese armourer, dates from around 1450.

KNIGHT IN 'GOTHIC' ARMOUR
end of fifteenth century

28
Knight in 'Maximilian' Armour
beginning of sixteenth century

By the end of the fifteenth and the beginning of the sixteenth century, armourers' workshops had proliferated throughout Europe; Germany and Italy were no longer the only centres of manufacture. European rulers took into their service Italian and German armourers, who brought with them the latest technological and stylistic innovations. Among the best known of the new centres were London (Greenwich), Ipswich and Southwark in England; Paris, Tours, Lyons, Bordeaux and Valenciennes in France; Bruges, Antwerp, Ghent and Tournai in Flanders, and Seville, Burgos and Calatayud in Spain.

The first three decades of the sixteenth century saw the widespread use of armour with radially disposed grooves (flutings or crestings); this was called 'Maximilian' armour, but the name was sometimes taken to mean any armour of the period, thus blurring distinctions. In any case, there is no evidence that Emperor Maximilian I (1493–1519) was responsible for its creation or use, although he did take a practical interest in the production of armour (he founded the court workshop at Innsbruck in 1504) and the intricate engravings of Burgkmair of Treitzsaurwein.

It seems beyond doubt that the armour was created by fusion of the German and Italian styles, but it is not clear whether the intention was to strengthen the plates or to follow fashion. The fluting probably had its roots in the 'rippled' surface style of gothic armour. By about 1510, this had developed into real fluting, which sometimes covered the whole suit. Fluted armour seems to have gone out of fashion in Italy by about 1520, but remained in use in Germany until the next decade. Smooth-surface armour, however, was as popular during Maximilian's reign as the fluted variant; indeed, outside Germany, it was the most universal.

Armour of the beginning of the sixteenth century used larger plates to cover the joints of the limbs, which had been the weak point of the gothic style; and the helmet no longer rested on the head but on the shoulders. The beginning of that century also brought about an important innovation: pieces of exchange or double pieces. These were bits of armour which reinforced the original construction, or which could be exchanged to alter the original shape for various purposes.

Shortly after the turn of the century, large bards became fashionable throughout Europe, and remained in vogue until the mid-century. Horse-armour was decorated too, of course, and its decoration clung closely to patterns used for the knights' armour. In Germany, special helmets for horses taking part in jousts and tournaments were produced: they had no visors, so the horses effectively ran blind. This innovation was probably intended to prevent the horses from turning away from each other.

KNIGHT IN 'MAXIMILIAN' ARMOUR
beginning of sixteenth century

29
Herald
first half of sixteenth century

In biblical times the word herald meant messenger or announcer. In feudal European courts they were responsible for court ceremony and proclamations, and for the organization of tournaments and jousts. Heralds, together with priests, were among the few people who could read and write, and as they spent their lives at court, witnessing history at first hand, they were entrusted with recording it. Large and powerful feudal families had their own heralds, who recorded their annals.

By the middle of the twelfth century, the protection of warriors had got to the stage where the mail hauberk covered the body, and the helmet, called a great helm, the head. In the confusion of battle, it was almost impossible to tell friend from foe, because everybody's equipment was similar and the faces were covered. For this reason, knights and nobles began painting various pictures and devices on their shields, to facilitate recognition. At first, these markings were decorative, but the heralds soon realized that if they were systematized, and if each knight were to use a unique and distinctive shield, everyone (and the heralds in particular) would be able to tell who was who.

It would seem that a system widely adopted by the Norman aristocracy was developed by the heralds by the early thirteenth century, and from then on the court heralds controlled it. A new duty was added: design and recording of coats-of-arms, and advising upon matters pertaining to them. The whole system was dubbed heraldry.

According to heraldic rules, three elements were needed for the composition of each coat-of-arms: tincture, shield and charge. The tinctures used were divided into metals and colours. The metals are or, meaning gold, but usually represented by yellow, and argent, meaning silver, but usually denoted by white. The colours are gules (scarlet), azure (blue), vert (green), purpure (purple), tenne (orange), sanguine (dark red), sable (black) and occasionally furs (the colour of ermine fur).

The shield is the surface on which the coat-of-arms is represented, and the shape used is a war shield. The simple shield has only one colour or metal, while a complex one is divided by lines into several parts.

Anything represented on the shield, whatever its form or nature, is a charge. The oldest, and simplest, charges were usually plain geometrical forms. These are called ordinaries. Later coats-of-arms used various motifs: animal, plant, mythological, biblical, celestial, and so on.

Coats-of-arms were placed on clothes, equipment, dishes, walls – anywhere where they could point out the dignity, position and importance of the owner. Heralds were dressed in liveries with their masters' arms, and in their colours. In processions and parades, they went at the front, thus announcing the arrival of their masters.

HERALD
first half of sixteenth century

30
Knight in Tournament Armour
beginning of sixteenth century

The origins of the medieval tournament are still mysterious. They were possibly derived from the Roman *Ludus Trojae*, in which two groups of warriors engaged in a sham battle. The word tournament, it should be noted, should properly be used only to denote such pretended combat between two groups of contestants; when two individual warriors compete, the correct word is joust.

Tournaments – public competitions among knights – were organized by kings and important feudal lords for public celebrations. The first took place in France in the ninth century, and soon afterwards the fashion spread to Germany, England and even Byzantium. The number of participants was unlimited: there could be up to 2,000, and tournaments could last for days. The first rules were set down in the ninth century by French knight Geoffroy de Preuilly. In the beginning, it seems that ordinary armour and weapons were used for both jousts and tournaments, so they could have differed very little from the real thing. It was only in the second half of the thirteenth century that armour made especially for that purpose came into general use.

Tournaments were usually held on large, flat fields in front of castles. The rectangular combat area was fenced in, and the spectators sat around it. Important personalities and the judges were usually seated on the castle's balconies, or special stands and tents were erected for them. Individual combat came first, then fighting in pairs, and finally in groups. At a sign, the contestants, mounted on their horses, swathed in sumptuous capes and armed with so-called courtesy weapons (lances without points, swords with dull blades and blunted maces) entered the arena, while heralds announced their names. They had previously been inspected by the judges. Occasionally, real weapons were used. Combat generally ceased when one of the contestants was struck from his saddle, but could continue until one of the opponents could no longer put up any resistance. The winners were given awards by the queen or one of the high-ranking ladies, and gained enormous prestige.

Severe injuries and accidental killings were frequent, so the pope and kings often forbade tournaments, especially at times of Crusades, but they were organized in spite of the bans. To decrease the number of injuries, a longitudinal barrier separating the combatants was introduced. After 1559, when Henri II of France was killed in a tournament after being accidentally struck in the eye through his visor by an opponent's lance, tournaments were held only in Germany, until the mid-seventeenth century. From the middle of the sixteenth century, dexterity and elegance were more appreciated than strength, and this contributed to the replacement of tournaments by attractive equestrian shows – carousels.

Cavalry forces often held competitions with some of the characteristics of tournaments: cutting down markers, snatching rings with lances, shooting from horseback at full gallop, and so on. In many countries, there are still different equestrian games with elements of medieval tournaments.

KNIGHT IN TOURNAMENT ARMOUR
beginning of sixteenth century

31
Spanish Ginete
beginning of sixteenth century

In 1492, Christopher Columbus discovered the island now known as Cuba, named it Hispaniola, and claimed it for the Spanish crown. Nineteen years later, Hernán Cortés, Spanish nobleman and officer, landed on Hispaniola, to serve in the local garrison. In 1518, with 570 men, 10 cannon and 16 horses, he invaded Mexico and began the conquest of a vast, hitherto unknown area, the Aztec Empire. The horses used had been brought across the Atlantic from Spain, from the southern province of Andalusia, known for raising breeds of mixed European, north African and Arabian origin. Cortés's expedition had 11 studs (two of them pintos) and five mares.

The horses belonged to some of the officers and the light horsemen known as *ginetes* or *genitors*, after their characteristic heart-shaped Moorish leather-covered shields. Their main weapons were swords and javelins, but some also carried crossbows. Some had plate armour, but most used mail shirts or brigantines (armour consisting of small plates fastened to the inside of a fabric covering), a steel cap (*morion* – type of Spanish kettle-hat) and some leg and arm protection. Officers wore three-quarter armour and open helmets. Their horses were unprotected.

By 1521, Cortés had broken the resistance of the natives (whom he called Indians) by plunder, massacres and the cunning use of firearms and especially of the horses, which had previously been unknown to the Aztecs. The following year, with the help of reinforcements which brought his army to 850 men, 15 cannon and 86 horses, he conquered the territories of present-day Honduras and Guatemala, and was appointed governor of the newly acquired areas, which were named Nueva España (New Spain). The Spanish conquest did not stop there. In 1533, Francisco Pizarro, at the head of 180 men, two cannons and 27 horses brought down the Inca Empire in Peru, and in 1538 Gonzez de Jeliauesada conquered Colombia.

Although they were constantly at war, the Spaniards and the Indians had one aim in common: the Spaniards wanted to raise as many horses as possible, the Indians to capture them and do the same. However carefully the Spaniards guarded their horses, the Mexican Indians were soon mounted. In 1598, the expedition led by Juan de Onante through the territory of modern New Mexico up to the present border of Kansas, sighted not a single horse in the area. Fifty years later, all the tribes of the western plains were mounted; the best known being the Apache and Comanche. The Indians especially prized pinto horses, so if a horse had no natural pattern, one was often painted on.

SPANISH GINETE
beginning of sixteenth century

32
German Reiter
mid-sixteenth century

Towards the middle of the sixteenth century, Thuringian Count Günter of Schwartzburg created the Schwarzern Reitern (Black Horsemen). It was a modern cavalry unit, stressing firepower and agility. *Reiter* or *ritter* meant only 'rider', but it became the generic name for the mercenary, partly armoured cavalrymen recruited in Germany in the 1550s, and later, during the Wars of Religion, in Spain, Italy and France.

These reiters (*swarte rutters* to the English) were also hired by Henry VIII. They were armoured cavalrymen, but rode unarmoured horses. Their principal weapon was a boar-spear – a broad-bladed spear, 2½–3 m/8–9 ft in length, with usually a small transverse bar below the blade. They also carried wheel-lock pistols, a German invention which soon replaced the spear, especially in the second half of the century, and became a symbol of the reiters. They played an important part in European warfare until the end of the sixteenth century.

The formation most often used by the reiters was the squadron of 300 or 400 men. Their preferred battle formation was the closed-order block, with 20 to 30 ranks. This deep formation enabled the men in the rear to reload after having discharged their weapons at the enemy and filed off to the flank and rear, allowing the next group to do so. This procedure was repeated until their opponents were sufficiently weakened to create conditions for a charge, when thrusting swords and clubbed pistols came into action.

The armour used by the reiters was not uniform and could vary from just a mail shirt or cape, through corselet (often with mail sleeves), to three-quarter armour. Helmets ranged from simple 'iron-hats' to *burgonets* or *morions*. They were armed with large pistols of the *faustrohre* type (*faust* – hand, *rohre* – barrel), thus named because they were as well suited for clubbing as for shooting the enemy. It had a barrel length of about 50 cm/20 in, weighed about 3 kg/6.5 lb and fired a 30 g/1 oz lead ball. The pistol could be aimed accurately from approximately 20 paces; unaimed fire could be effective up to 45 m/50 yds. However, it was effective against the most heavily armoured opponents only at a few paces.

A reiter was usually armed with two or three pistols: two carried in holsters on his saddle bow, and the third, precariously, in his right boot. There were, however, mercenary companies where reiters had up to six pistols – four in holsters, and one in each boot. Their armour was often blackened; a common measure to fight rust. However, it was also the source of the name *schwarz reiter*, as well as of the French *diables noirs*.

GERMAN REITER
mid-sixteenth century

33
Mounted Arquebusier
sixteenth century

The arquebus was a firearm directly descended from fourteenth-century handguns. There are two theories about the name, which comes from the German *hakenbuchsen* (hook-gun in translation). The first arquebuses were about 2 m/6.5 ft long and weighed up to 30 kg/65 lb; as they were used mainly from fortress walls, they were hooked to the parapet at the front of the barrel, the better to take the recoil. The other explanation relies for evidence on lighter weapons (5–7 kg/11–15 lb), which had hook-shaped butts.

The lighter arquebuses from the beginning of the sixteenth century had wooden butts made from walnut, birch or maple. Barrel length was about 1.5 m/5 ft, calibre 12–20 mm. At first they were made of bronze, but later of iron. The lock was simple: an S-shaped vice held the match (cord soaked in saltpetre solution), and dropped it into the firing-pan of the gun. Balls were at first stone, then lead, iron, and, in the case of rifled arquebuses, iron covered with sheepskin or lead. Loading was complicated, and even the most skilled marksmen could get off only 40 shots an hour at best, but was simplified with the introduction of the bandolier, which had a number of wooden cases (usually 12; colloquially called the 12 apostles) hanging from it. Each case contained powder for one shot. Priming powder was carried in a horn or flask, and the bullets separately. At first, it took two men to service an arquebus; later, one man could do so.

The best German weapons had a maximum range of about 400 paces. However, the effective range in battle was much smaller, let alone the range at which some semblance of accuracy could be achieved. The arquebus was popular, though because, despite being cumbersome, it had a greater penetrating power than the bow or crossbow.

The same reasons which led to the creation of units of mounted archers or crossbowmen resulted in the appearance of mounted *arquebusiers*. Their weapons were of higher quality and smaller, to enable handling, and their role in combat, whether mounted or on foot, was to prepare and support attacks with their fire.

Arquebusiers usually fought from a distance, so they had no need of heavy armour. Initially, they used helmets, breast- and back-plates and protection for the arms and thighs. In the sixteenth and seventeenth centuries, these pieces of armour were discarded one by one, until only the helmet remained. They wore a long straight sword for personal defence, like the rest of the heavy cavalry. The arquebusiers of mercenary companies, however, were veritable arsenals on horseback: besides the arquebus, they carried up to six pistols in holsters and stuck into their belts.

The picture shows an arquebusier in the dress of the *pferdschützenharnisch*. Breastplates, when worn, had a pointed medial ridge – the *tauplbrust* – to encourage shots to ricochet.

MOUNTED ARQUEBUSIER
sixteenth century

34
English
Demi-lancer

c. 1550

In the period between the Hundred Years War (1339–1453) and the English Civil Wars (1642–8) the English army stagnated relative to the armed forces of the Continent. The technology of manufacture and quality of weapons lagged behind the European centres. Waging war was expensive, and this was reflected most in the cavalry. A contemporary wrote that in all of Wales only a few good horses could be found. In 1544, King Henry VIII (1509–47) organized a campaign in France, accompanied by 73 fully armoured 'gentleman pensioners' of the Household Cavalry, and 121 heavily armoured men-at-arms. The rest of the 4,000 English cavalry were English gentry who served as demi-lances on unbarded horses, light horsemen called 'Light Staves' and 'Javelins' and the Scottish 'Border Horse'. European kings of Henry's rank could summon many thousand heavy cavalrymen, compared to his several hundred.

One of Henry's first undertakings had been the reorganization and replenishing of the national arsenal. In 1512, 2,000 complete harnesses of the *almayne ryvettes* type were bought from Florentine merchant Guido Portinari. These were similar to the armour worn by the German Landsknecht. Each set included a helmet (*sallet*), throat protector (*gorget*), backplate, breastplate and a pair of arm harnesses. All this was obtained at the favourable price of 16 shillings a set, and a further 5,000 sets were bought in Milan the following year.

After special armour for the infantry was introduced, similar protection for medium and light cavalry became the norm. Medium cavalry in England were known as lances or demi-lances, and used a lighter type of lance which did not require the use of a lance-rest. In modern parlance, their armour was of the three-quarters type (German *harnash*), because it extended to the knees only. From the mid-sixteenth century, the demi-lances started using the morion helmet, previously popular among the infantry.

After 1550, the term 'light horse' seems to have been widespread, but it did not refer to the demi-lances. It seems that light horse troops wore a cuirass with no lance-rest, an open helmet, and optional mail sleeves. On occasion, the cuirass was replaced with only a mail shirt. Gauntlets and an oval shield were also in use. The English demi-lances used heavier horses (another reason why they were not included in the light horse), and their chief role was in a set battle, making them a cheaper substitute for battle cavalry.

In the 1660s, the demi-lances, who made up about one-fifth of the English cavalry, increasingly rejected the lance and started using firearms – pistols, arquebuses and petronels (sixteenth-century cavalry gun of medium size).

ENGLISH DEMI-LANCER
c. 1550

35
Hungarian Hussar
fifteenth–sixteenth
century

Hungarian archives contain a pay list from the second half of the fifteenth century, covering men whom military officials recruited for the army of King Matthias I Corvinus (1458–90). It describes a light horseman armed with a long lance, sword and composite bow, riding on a high eastern saddle (taken from the Avars), dressed in colourful Renaissance costume with plumes and with a teardrop-shaped shield in his left hand. The legend is 'hussar'.

Riders fitted out like the hussar were around even earlier, not only in Hungary but in Poland, Lithuania, Bohemia and other eastern countries, although nowhere else were these men referred to by a special name. In Hungary the name hussar was probably also applied to any soldier called up under feudal rule by the Hungarian king. However, during the rule of Matthias Corvinus, hussar meant one particular and easily recognizable type of horseman, organized in units called hussar units. The name later spread to neighbouring states.

There are several hypotheses about the origin of the name hussar. One attributes it to the Avars, another to the name used to denote soldiers in Byzantium. Many historians, however, believe that the root of the name is in the Hungarian word *husz*, meaning twenty. When the king called, the nobility had to equip one soldier for every 20 able-bodied serfs. The same applied to the free royal cities, and to the fishermen on the Danube, who provided men for the royal navy.

Later on, Matthias replaced the unreliable feudal army with a more loyal mercenary force. Together with the Bohemian infantry and German armoured cavalry, the most numerous were the Hungarian light horsemen, so the former name from the feudal obligation was transferred to the Hungarian light cavalry, the hussars.

There was not another country in Europe whose history and destiny were so closely tied to horses and riders as ancient Hungary. This territory, now known as the Pannonian valley (and once called the Portal of Europe) saw the westward passage of Huns, Avars, Magyars, Tartars and Cumans, all of whom left many traces of their warrior and riding skills. Hungary, without any major natural obstacles, could be conquered or defended on horseback only, so, life in those parts was linked with equestrian skills. This strongly influenced the appearance and behaviour of the hussars.

HUNGARIAN HUSSAR
fifteenth–sixteenth century

36
Stradiotti
Light Cavalryman
sixteenth century

In the fifteenth century Venice was a rich city-republic, and gained control of the eastern shores of the Adriatic thanks to its position and to powerful merchant and battle navies. After the conquest of Constantinople by the Turks in 1453 and the consequent fall of the Byzantine Empire, Venice captured many islands in the Aegean and consolidated its hold in the eastern Adriatic. Being rich, it could maintain a professional army which kept its neighbours at bay. At the height of its power, the republic had 200,000 citizens, and ruled an area inhabited by 2.5 million people.

As the Ottomans drove further west, Venice was faced with raids by Akinci, Deli and Tartar light horsemen which it could not successfully combat. In 1470, the services of Greek and Albanian *stradiotti* or *estradiotti* light horsemen (*stradiotos* – Greek for soldier) were engaged. These men knew the tactics of the Turkish riders, because they fought the same way themselves.

They were organized into units of between 100 and 300 men, and detailed to garrison towns which lay on possible routes of Turkish incursions. The stradiotti were mobile and fast and acted suddenly and decisively, so they carried out reconnaissance as well as border protection.

Later on, under the name stradiots, Venice and other Italian states (Milan, Siena, Pisa, Genoa) took into service Croats and Hungarians. Hunyadi Janos and Miklos Zriny and their troops were mercenaries in wars on Italian soil. At the Battle of Fornovo (1495), 2,000 stradiots attacked from the rear and destroyed the supply train of the French army. At Agandello (1509), the largest cavalry unit was 3,000 stradiots, and at Pavia (1525), 500 stradiots attacked the French position from the left wing and contributed to victory.

Italian states which could not afford their services had to compensate in other ways – for example, in 1480 Naples hired 1,500 Turkish light horsemen – and the Spaniards employed *ginetes* of Moorish origin, although in 1507 they too engaged the services of 1,000 stradiots.

Their equipment and armament was a mixture of eastern and western. Only the Croats wore a local type of broadsword called the *sciavona*. Full armament consisted of a long lance, eastern composite bow and sabre or sword. Use of a shield and other protective gear was optional and helmets, mail coif and some parts of body-armour were not unknown.

A large number of light horsemen, known as hussars in eastern Europe, took part in the Italian wars of the sixteenth century, although they were rarely mentioned by this name. It seems that the term stradiot had become a synonym for eastern mercenary light cavalry in Italy.

STRADIOTTI LIGHT CAVALRYMAN
sixteenth century

37
Parade Armour
c. 1560

When Maximilian armour came into use, in the late fifteenth and early sixteenth centuries, its decoration also came into vogue, picked up from everyday late-Renaissance life, when nearly everything was ornamented. Cavalry armour was manufactured in three distinct variants: war, tournament and parade.

Parade armour was either very similar to war armour or copied ancient models. It was made from thinner plates, so that it could be more easily worked with various tools and worn with greater comfort. Armour was decorated using various techniques: engraving, etching, embossing, damascening, silvering, gilding and, oldest of all, painting. Engraving involved the cutting of decorative patterns into the armour with a sharply pointed tool. Etching produced the same results, but with the use of acid. Before etching, the parts of the armour not to be decorated were covered with a protective coating of wax or paint. The uncovered areas were eaten by the acid, to give the desired patterns. Embossing consisted of hammering the plates, resulting in concave or convex ornaments. Damascening was the encrustation or inlaying of gold or silver into depressions in the armour's surface, silvering the covering of its complete surface with silver foil on a hatched ground. In gilding, an amalgam of copper and zinc was applied by the use of heat. The German technique of *goldschmeltz*, also widely used in weapons' decoration, was similar to gilding: the foundation was coppered and filled with an amalgam of mercury and gold. The plate was then heated until the mercury dispersed, leaving the gold adhering to the design. The armour was subsequently polished until the gold was flush with the surface. Armour was protected from rust by heating, which gave it the characteristic blued or blackened colour.

Parade armour was an important element of court ceremony, and a symbol of knighthood in the social life of the nobility. For the occasion of the marriage of the Duke of Brunswick and Hedwig of Brandenburg in 1560, announced two years in advance, over 100 suits of parade armour were made for clients from the Spanish, Austrian and German courts, including a few of children's armour! Manufacturers and artisans who carried out the ornamentation became famous throughout Europe. An album of pen and wash drawings of 45 harnesses decorated between 1546 and 1563 by the renowned Augsburg etcher Jörg Sorg (active 1517–64) has been preserved. The suits made for the Spanish noblemen, the Duke of Alva and Duke Garcia of Toledo, by Anton Peffenhauser (1525–1603) and for Maximilian II by Matthäus Frauenpress, all etched by Jörg Sorg, have also come down to us. And we can still admire the suit of armour of Emperor Charles V, etched by Giacomo Filippo (1531–61), one of the best-known Milanese craftsmen to use this technique.

The illustration shows an embossed and burnished suit of parade half-armour made in Innsbruck by Kunz Lochner the Younger (1510–67).

PARADE ARMOUR

c. 1560

38
Turkish Sipahi
fifteenth–sixteenth century

In the military structure of the Ottoman Empire, feudal cavalrymen were granted fiefs, with the proviso that they were personally obliged to answer a call to war, bringing their own equipment and horse, or to send a stand-in with a certain number of men, depending on the size of the fief and the income derived from it. The *sipahi* who did not fulfil his military obligations lost his fief.

Smaller fiefs, providing incomes from 1,000 to 20,000 *akchy* (Turkish silver currency), were called *timar*, while those producing from 20,000 to 100,000 were called *zeamete*; their lords were called *timargi* or *zaim* respectively. A completely armed horseman (*gebeli*) had to be provided for every 3,000 akchy by a timargi or every 5,000 by a zaim. The gebelis were recruited mainly from slaves and prisoners, or were bought by the sipahi, like the Mamelukes in Egypt. Because of the personal gain they derived from campaigns, sipahis were known to equip more gebelis than they needed. After the death of a sipahi, part of his fief was inherited by his sons, and part could be inherited by his gebelis, who thus became sipahis in their own right.

From the fifteenth century, in countries under Turkish rule, there were Christian feudals who became Turkish sipahis. In the Bosnian *sancak* (an administrative unit of the Empire), there were 111 Christian timars in 1469. In 1476, in the Smederevo sancak, there were more Christian than Muslim sipahis, and there were about 3,000 in Herzegovina at the beginning of the sixteenth century. This number continued to grow, and the sipahis from these areas played prominent roles on the battlefields of Europe, Asia and Africa. When Ottoman feudalism grew stronger, most of these had to convert to Islam to preserve their timars; those who did not were edged out, and finally disappeared completely.

Sipahis were the mainstay of the provincial army (*elayet*), and the most numerous of the Ottoman armed forces; there were about 40,000 of them in the sixteenth century. Their units were called *alay*, each with 1,000 men, and they were commanded by an *alay-bey*, who reviewed his sipahis before going to war according to a register (*defter*) of feudal holdings. Every tenth sipahi remained at home to keep the peace and do the work of those who had gone to war.

The cavalry elite of the Ottoman army – about 6,000 men – was in the six sipahi units of the sultan's household cavalry (*alti boluk*): the left wing and right wing salaried men (*ulufeciyan*), the left wing and right wing poor foreigners (*querba*), the weapon bearers (*silathar*), and the elite of the elite, the sipahi children (*sipahi oglan*). Units had differently coloured pennants on their lances.

TURKISH SIPAHI
fifteenth–sixteenth century

39
Mounted Samurai
sixteenth century

In the early history of Japan, the *samurai* were members of the court guard. In the eighth century, with the development of feudal relations, they became vassals of the larger feudal lords, the barons (*daimyo*) and served as their armed escort, or served the emperor directly. This is the root of their name, *samurau* meaning to serve.

The drawn-out feudal struggles among the great lords, which began in the twelfth century, loosened the bonds of imperial authority, but also made the samurai influential, turning them into a privileged military caste. Most were tied to the feudal lords, who did not give them land holdings but paid them in kind. The most privileged of the samurai were the bannermen (*hatamoto*), vassals of the *shogun*, militarily the strongest feudal lord in Japan, who was the country's true ruler; the emperor was no more than a figurehead. The task of the hatamoto was to go to war for the shogun and, in times of peace, to oversee his holdings and collect taxes.

The strict code of the *bushido* (way of the warrior) defined the basic moral qualities of the samurai: loyalty to his master, disdain towards the lower social classes, seeking out danger, moderation, and rejection of women and money. The highest expression of the readiness to self-denial was the obligation to commit suicide in certain situations: if the master ordered it as punishment for mistakes made, in order to avoid capture, to protest against abuses of power, and to warn the master against actions which might be harmful to his reputation or interests. The bushido was founded on ancient Chinese philosophy and Buddhism.

Until the bloody civil war of 1550–1615, battles in the Japanese wars resembled individual clashes, similar to the knightly duels in Europe. The difference was that in Japan duels were often fought with large bows, both on foot and from the saddle. To shoot the bow from the saddle, the rider had to hold it in its lower third, because of its size, and to facilitate this operation, bows were made in asymmetrical shapes. They were made of laminated wood and bound with rattan. Nowadays, at the traditional archery event in the town of Kamakura, participants demonstrate the art of shooting a bow from a horse in full gallop (*yabusame*), used in combat by the samurai several centuries ago.

Until the thirteenth or fourteenth century, archery combat was the principal form of horseback fighting; swordplay was marginal. When fighting on horseback, the samurai used a long, single-handed sword (*tachi*). As sword combat became more important, fighting on foot increased, and the samurai used a shorter, two-handed sword (*katana*).

During the civil war, large armies were raised which fought rationally and purposefully; there was less and less space for the traditional forms of combat. One of the most powerful warlords, Takeda Shingen (1521–73), organized an effective cavalry force which charged the enemy with spears and swords, and was also successful in hand-to-hand combat.

MOUNTED SAMURAI
sixteenth century

40
Muscovite Boyar
late sixteenth century

From the second half of the fifteenth century, a growing role in the Russian army was assigned to the nobility (*boyars*), who were bound to service by possession of fiefs. This system in the armed forces became particularly strong during the rule of Ivan IV ('the Terrible', 1530–84). Reforms carried out in the mid-sixteenth century tied the small nobility to the emperor (*tzar*) by the granting of fiefs. These men were the foundation for increasing absolutism. As early as 1550, a special caste of nobles under military obligation was formed; 1,078 of them were given land around Moscow, and these were the 'chosen one thousand', landowners directly dependent on the emperor. Army officers were recruited from among their ranks; nobles under military obligation from other parts of the country, who were the majority, held subordinate positions and were called 'city obligators'.

Noblemen made up the cavalry, which numbered about 25,000 towards the end of the sixteenth century; in times of war, this could increase to 40–50,000. In appearance, Russian cavalry followed the eastern pattern. Mail or plate armour was worn, with eastern-type helmets and forearm vambraces; retainers did not have this protective equipment, but wore padded clothes which could stop an arrow. Fur and silk and jewels were worn, while the armour was richly ornamented with inlays; sometimes, the mail was made of silver. Weapons included lances, javelins, scimitars, maces, and, in the late sixteenth century, pistols. The principal weapon, however, was the composite bow.

Russian cavalrymen rode jockey-style, with knees drawn up, which largely determined their tactics. This position was ideal for the archer, but unsuited to receiving a lance blow. Russian horses were wiry, but small, and this was another reason for the avoidance of frontal charges. Tactics were surprise and numerical superiority, which enabled them to surround the enemy and fire from a distance, avoiding close combat. Discipline was somewhat lacking, but the men were loosely organized into squadrons (100) and regiments (1,000). Several regiments made up a division (*polk*), of which there were six: van (*perodovoi polk*), left (*levoi polk*) and right (*pravoi polk*) wings, main body (*bolsoi polk*), reserve (*smorozevoi polk*) and a kind of light cavalry unit detached forward for skirmishing and reconnaissance (*ermaulni polk*). Each division had its own pennant of St George.

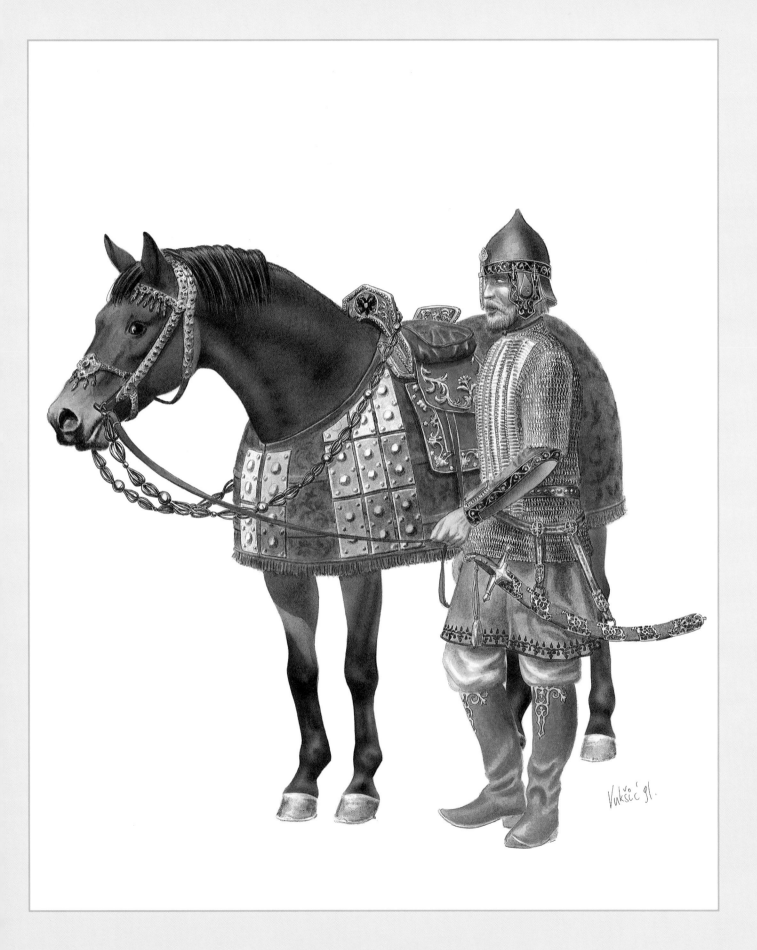

MUSCOVITE BOYAR
late sixteenth century

41
Wallachian
Cavalryman
c. 1575

The original occupants of what is now known as Romania called themselves Vlachs (not to be confused with a similar word used in Serbia and Bulgaria for cattle-raisers), and formed three independent states: Wallachia about 1324, Moldavia in 1359 and Transylvania at the beginning of the fifteenth century. First they were vassals of Hungary, later battlegrounds for the interests of Hungary, Poland, Austria and Turkey. At the beginning of the fifteenth century, the Ottoman Turks appeared on the borders of Wallachia, which finally fell under their rule in 1526, after the Battle of Mohacs. Prince Vlad Tepes the Impaler (1418–56) (also known as Count Dracula) gained notoriety through his cruelty in the struggle against the Turks, and it was from him that the Turks learned to impale their prisoners on stakes without killing them at once, a skill they were later to use extensively. After the Turkish occupation, the Vlachs shared the fate of all occupied peoples. The local feudal lords (*hospodars*) often rose against the Turks, and took to the mountains and woods with their armed bands.

In equipment and appearance, the Vlachs were similar to the Hungarians and Russians; they wore large fur capes decorated with feathers, and sported the characteristic long, rounded beards. After their victory over the Turks at Calugareni in 1595, Vlach armies became almost completely cavalry forces. Several contemporary engravings by de Bruyn, made between 1575 and 1581, help us to reconstruct the appearance of the Wallachian cavalrymen.

They belonged, for the most part, to a type of light cavalry (*calarasi*), who acquired much of their equipment and equestrian skills from the Ottomans. Besides training their horses to walk, trot and gallop, the Vlachs taught them to walk like camels, moving both legs on one side at the same time. Today one can find horses walking that way, but it is considered a bad trait.

From the end of the sixteenth century, Wallachians served as mercenary horsemen to both the Ottoman Empire and its enemies – Poland, Hungary and Russia. They were organized in squadrons (*sotnia*, from the Russian word for 100) of about one hundred men. At one time there were 20 sotnias in Polish service in the Ukraine, and one of the frequent motifs on their flags was a bull's head. Like the Ottomans, they refused to use firearms for a long time; their main weapons were spear, sabre and composite bow. For protection, they wore mail shirts and used a light round shield.

WALLACHIAN CAVALRYMAN
c. 1575

42
Imperialist
Cuirassier
c. 1630

After 41 years of war, peace was made between Spain and the Netherlands in 1609. Part of the rich Dutch provinces had liberated themselves from Spanish rule and gained independence: the small professional Dutch army, commanded by Maurice of Nassau, stood against a world power. The most significant changes in the Dutch War of Independence were implemented in the cavalry. In 1597, out of a total of 11 ensigns of lancers (1,200 men in all), eight were converted to pistol-armed cuirassiers, and three to arquebusiers. The heaviest cavalry units rejected the lance in favour of firearms. The same year, at the Battle of Turnhout, the Dutch cavalry, practically on their own, routed Spanish cuirassiers armed with lances and infantry with long pikes.

From the Dutch border to Poland on the west and Turkey to the south were the semi-independent states dominated by the Austrian Habsburg dynasty. This whole area of central Europe, known for centuries as the Holy Roman Empire, was ruled from Vienna by the Austrian emperor, and the soldiers in his service were called simply 'imperialists'. To distinguish themselves from other soldiers, they wore a red sash around their waists or over their shoulders and an oak twig in their helmets or hats.

At the turn of the century, imitating their Dutch counterparts, the imperial cuirassiers abandoned the heavy lance and began to use a pair of pistols. More reliable and lighter firearms were one factor which would shape their future strategy; another was the formation of infantry units several thousand men strong, half armed with muskets and arquebuses, the rest protecting them from heavy cavalry attacks with six-metre pikes.

In the early seventeenth century, the imperial works began producing armour which discarded all superfluous parts but strengthened the back- and breastplates and headgear. Because of the materials used, cavalry armour became heavier and more massive. The heaviest models extant today are on show in the Landeszeughaus museum in Graz; they weigh 42 kg/90 lb. Their surface is unornamented, and their form not as refined as in previous phases: protection of the wearer against the improved firearms was paramount.

Cuirassiers played a prominent role in the Thirty Years War, commanded by Field Marshal Gottfried Pappenheim (1594–1632) and Albrecht Wallenstein (1583–1634). Pappenheim formed up his cuirassier regiments, about 1,000 men strong, in ten files of 100 men, stressing depth and narrowing the front. Wallenstein, on the other hand, disposed his units, of about the same strength, in six ranks emphasizing the initial strike over a wide front; his method was more successful.

IMPERIALIST CUIRASSIER

c. 1630

43
Dragoon

c. 1630

In one of the numerous Italian wars between 1552 and 1559 the French army occupied Piedmont. Threatened by Spanish troops, French Marshal de Brissac ordered his bravest infantry arquebusiers and musketeers on to horseback. He thus achieved a kind of mechanized infantry, which used horses only for transport, and fought on foot, like ordinary infantry. In the seventeenth century, other states followed this example and formed mounted infantry units, naming them dragoons. One story of the name's origin has the French giving one of these new units a dragon pennant, frequently used in Byzantium and the Carolingian state. Another theory traces it to the word for a short-barrelled musket-bore firelock: the *dragon*.

The first dragoon regiments were organized during the Thirty Years War (1618–48) although the Dutch had dragoons as early as 1606, and the Swedes in 1611. Their organization and armament were practically identical to infantry units. In cavalry units, the men, called troopers, were divided into squadrons, each having a standardbearer and trumpeter; dragoon privates served in companies and battalions with guidon bearers and drumboys. In the beginning, the first three companies of a regiment were named in the same way as in the infantry – colonel's, lieutenant-colonel's and major's. Dragoon regiments usually had 10 to 15 companies, each with approximately 100 men, which made them stronger than their real cavalry namesakes, which rarely had more than 500 troopers.

In the first decades of the seventeenth century, dragoon uniforms were little different from those of infantry musketeers. The shoes and stockings were replaced with boots and spurs, and a helmet sometimes substituted for the hat, but that hardly equipped them for a cavalry battle; in addition, only the officers had pistols, while the men had firelock muskets, unsuited to fighting on horseback. Every dragoon carried a sword, and his equipment included a small pick which could be used for tethering the horse when they operated on foot. It is interesting to note that the Austrian imperial dragoons had armoured pikemen and officers with halberds until 1625. Dragoons' mounts were small and cheap, and could not stand up to real cavalry horses. Occasionally, dragoons were trained to shoot from horseback; even less frequently, they mounted charges.

The Swedish dragoons seem to have been an exception: their main role was providing fire support for the cavalry, and they rarely dismounted in battle.

DRAGOON
c. 1630

44
Croat
1630

The Ottoman onslaught on Europe lost momentum towards the end of the sixteenth century, and came to halt in upper Hungary and Croatia, in the area known as *militargränze* (military border), the rulers in Vienna having organized their external line of defence on the territory of Croatia towards the end of the fifteenth century. When Turkish incursions into Croatian territory became more frequent, the Croatian nobility moved into the fortified towns on the border and began strengthening them.

In 1527, Austrian Archduke Ferdinand I was elected Croatian king, and pledged to the Croatian *sabor* (assembly) that he would station 1,000 cavalrymen and 200 infantry in Croatia, the first standing forces to be permanently stationed there. The incessant Turkish raids were ruining the border areas: their populations were being taken into slavery, and whole regions were suffering economic collapse. Austria resettled these areas with people who had fled the Turks – Serbs, Hungarians, Romanians and Wallachians – who assumed an obligation of permanent military service by all males from 18 to 60. Some served in permanent units of the *vojna krajina* (military border), others in the people's militia. In return for their service, they were given houses and land, and were exempt from paying taxes. The standing army of the krajina was made up of Croatian nobles and the rest of the population. The cavalry units consisted of foreigners and large numbers of the domestic nobility. Even though it had become poor and had lost large parts of its territory, Croatia devoted significant resources to the defence of its borders, and the populace were permanently armed. Raids, ambushes, pillage and continuous war hardened these border warriors into merciless fighters devoted to the court of Vienna. Regardless of their origins, they were all known as Croats (German *croaten*).

They took part in wars all over Europe as part of the Austrian army, and fought as mercenaries in the Thirty Years War. Several regiments of Croats and Croat arquebusiers were organized, totalling aout 10,000 riders, mostly carrying firearms. In central and western Europe, the name became synonymous with light cavalry units consisting of Croats, Serbs and Hungarians, and even Poles, because by 1638 the number of Croat cavalry regiments had grown to 19, with 25,000–30,000 men, well beyond what Croatia alone could offer.

The Croats became famous in Europe for their skill, speed and bravery, but because of the tasks they were assigned (security, reconnaissance and diversions in the enemy's rear), they had to live off the land, and acquired a reputation as plunderers. In 1635, Louis XIII formed several regiments of Croats – the Royal Cravats.

CROAT
1630

45
Swedish
Medium
Cavalryman
1632

The Thirty Years War started in Germany in 1618; it was to bring imperial power and the Catholic reaction to their zenith. The appearance of imperial troops on the south shores of the Baltic and the aggressive Catholicism of Emperor Ferdinand II threatened Protestant Sweden. In July 1630, the Swedish warrior-king, Gustavus Adolphus, landed in Pomerania with a national army of 15,000 men and in two years had cleared most of Germany of imperial troops. At the moment of his death in the Battle of Lützen, in 1632, nearly 150,000 troops were fighting under the Swedish flag.

According to Clausewitz, Gustavus was a skilled military commander, inclined to cautious combinations, manoeuvres and systematic warfare; he was certainly a better organizer and tactician than strategist. Prior to the war with Germany, he honed his skills in the conflict with the Poles and their cavalry (1617–29). Following his rational views on warfare and tactics, he restructured the Swedish army to become the premier fighting force of the Continent and a model for reforms in other armed forces.

In this period, the battlefields of Europe were dominated by four types of horsemen, not counting the light oriental riders. The heaviest were the cuirassiers in three-quarter armour, whom Gustavus considered expensive relative to their performance; next were the light cavalry, partially armoured horsemen, who had a secondary role in combat and whom he considered unjustly neglected; he found the arquebusiers, with their fire support for cuirassiers and general gunnery action from horseback not offensive enough; and he thought that dragoons, the 'mounted infantry', could be put to better use.

The logical consequence of these opinions was a decision to make do with two types of horsemen: dragoons, who would take over the arquebusiers' role of fire support, and light horsemen, who would become his offensive cavalry. A few smaller cavalry units, mostly consisting of the Swedish nobility, were equipped with three-quarter cuirassier armour, but they did not affect the military operations and character of the king's cavalry.

In time, the standard Swedish cavalryman turned out to be of the so-called 'medium' type. He wore a corselet and a pot helmet (or large hat with skull-cap), and was armed with a pair of pistols and a sword somewhat longer than in other European armies. Tactics involved charging with drawn swords; only the first rank used firearms, and the salvo was delivered at point-blank range. On paper, the strength of a regiment was eight companies of 125 men each; in reality, regiments could have as few as four and as many as 12 companies.

Some of the best cavalrymen in the Swedish army were Finnish riders known as the *hakkapelis*, a name derived from their war-cry, which meant, 'Chop them down!'.

SWEDISH MEDIUM CAVALRYMAN
1632

46
Royalist (Cavalier)
1642

The immediate excuse for the beginning of the English Civil War between the feudal and bourgeois classes was disagreement over royal prerogatives and the rights of Parliament. The conflict between King Charles I (1600–49) and Parliament escalated because of the king's attempt to squeeze more money by levying new taxes without the approval of Parliament. There were also conflicts of interest over foreign and church policy.

In defence of his 'divine rights', Charles raised his standard at Nottingham in August 1642. Prince Rupert of the Rhine (1619–82) offered him eight troops of his Own Regiment of Horse, a total of about 500 men. Charles commissioned Prince Rupert as General of Horse.

Since 1618, the Thirty Years War had been blazing on the Continent, and Gustavus Adolphus had initiated a modern model of cavalry warfare, which had shown itself superior. Prince Rupert had served in the Swedish army, and brought these battle-tested ideas to England. The first clash took place on 23 September 1642, at Powick Bridge. At the head of his eight troops of horse and ten companies of dragoons, Rupert defeated ten troops of horse and five companies of dragoons of Essex's advance guard, inflicting 150 casualties. His cavaliers charged in the Swedish style, making use of the shock value and power of horses, and holding their fire until the mêlée. Their qualities notwithstanding, the royalist cavaliers had a tendency to slip from their officers' control once the battle had started, and be distracted from pursuit of the enemy by pursuit of the enemy's unprotected freight wagons. This proved fatal at the Battle of Naseby in 1645, which sunk all Charles's hopes for victory.

The English nobility, superb riders with military experience, were excellent material for Rupert's cavalry. After the Battle of Edgehill, in which the parliamentary cavalry was defeated, Oliver Cromwell, colonel of horse and Member of Parliament, wrote to Colonel John Hampden: 'The royalists' troopers are gentlemen's sons, younger sons and persons of quality; do you think that the spirits of such base and mean fellows [the parliamentary cavalry] will be ever able to encounter gentlemen that have honour courage and resolution in them…?'

Most of the royalist riders were equipped as light horsemen, according to continental standards. Their basic weapon was a long sword ('tuck'), but rapiers (for example, 'Pappenheimers') were also carried; two pistols – flintlocks or wheel-locks – were packed in saddle holsters. A buff coat was standard wear; armour consisted of a cuirass (corselet) and steel skull-cap worn underneath a hat. Royalists wore red or rose sashes. Their regiments had six to eight troops, with a total of about 300 cavaliers. On paper, the regiments were supposed to have about 500 men, but this was so only with elite units, such as those of the Earl of Forth, Lord Percy and Prince Maurice.

ROYALIST (CAVALIER)
1642

47
Ironside (Roundhead)
1645

In the English Civil War, the northern and western counties, mainly agricultural and dominated by the nobility, sided with the king, while the southern and eastern counties, where trade and industry had developed, backed Parliament. However, the cities in the north and west were for Parliament and the nobility in the south and east supported the king. In total six-sevenths of the population backed Parliament, which, supported by the bourgeoisie, had more money at its disposal and could afford a more effective mercenary army.

In his letter to Colonel Hampden after the defeat at Edgehill (see previous entry), Cromwell went on to say: 'Your troopers are most of them old decayed servingmen and tapsters and such kind of fellows... You must get men of a spirit that is likely to go as far as gentlemen will go, or else I am sure you will be beaten still...'

In the winter of 1644–5, Cromwell, who had become lieutenant-general of horse, began a reorganization of the army. Besides local county forces, new troops were recruited – infantry, and 7,000 cavalry, in 11 regiments of the New Model Army. Every regiment of horse had six troops of 100 men.

Cromwell's cavalry belonged to the type generally known as arquebusiers, which was misleading: the arquebus or carbine had almost been abandoned by this time. The men wore back- and breastplates over a buff leather coat and a helmet (the 'pot'), and were armed with swords and, sometimes, a small pole-axe. They carried only pistols, although it has been suggested that officers may have carried carbines in addition to the sword and pistols.

A trooper's pay was 2/- a day, in theory at least. However, he was expected to pay for food for himself and his mount, as well as for lodgings, clothing and horseshoes. A colonel's daily pay was 22/-, a major's 15/8d, a captain's 10/- and a lieutenant's 5/4d.

Good discipline was characteristic of the Ironsides; this nickname did not refer to their armour, but to their steadfastness and reliability in action. As individuals, they could not stand up to the cavaliers, but they were more effective as a fighting body. In battle, Cromwell kept his men under tight control, and did not let them disperse afterwards.

IRONSIDE (ROUNDHEAD)
1645

48
French
Mounted
Musketeer
1660

The musket was a hand-held firearm which first appeared in 1521 in Spain and in 1525 in France. It had a larger calibre than the arquebus (22–25 mm to 13–20 mm), a slightly longer barrel (up to 2 m/6.5 ft for the largest muskets) and weighed more – up to 10 kg/22 lb. The musket had greater penetration, but was more cumbersome and difficult to use. Two men were needed to operate Spanish muskets, which had to be braced on a forked rest. At the end of the sixteenth century, a musket could kill a man in 'shot-proof' armour at 10 paces, and a 'common armed man' at 20. A musket produced in 1580 in Styria (Austria) could fire a 50 g/1.8 oz, 20 mm-calibre ball at an angle of 60 degrees and to a distance of 1,500 m/1,600 yds; an accidental hit at several hundred paces could easily kill a man. Ninety-nine separate operations were required just for loading and preparation to fire this musket; a well-trained infantryman had to know a total of 143. The best marksmen of the period could hit a barn door at 200 paces.

French infantry was armed with lighter muskets from 1573, but arquebuses remained dominant until after the Thirty Years War. From 1620, smaller calibre muskets weighing up to 6 kg/13 lb were introduced.

King Henry IV of Navarre established France's regular army in 1597. In the 1600 reforms, he founded a company of his personal guard. These were gentlemen armed with carbines, and they were called Carabiniers du Roi. In 1622, Louis XII changed their carbines for the lighter muskets, and their name also changed, to Mousquetaires du Roi.

Louis XIV ascended the throne of France in 1643, when he was only five; until his coming of age, the country was ruled by Cardinal Mazarin, who had the musketeers under his patronage. In 1661, after the cardinal's death, Louis formed another company of 300 musketeers. The older ones were called the Mousquetaires Gris (grey), and the new troop the Mousquetaires Noirs (black), the colours corresponding to those of their horses' saddle-cloths.

The musketeers were described in Dumas's popular novel, *The Three Musketeers*. Its hero, D'Artagnan, was modelled on a real person, one Charles de Batz, who was killed during the Siege of Maastricht in 1673, at the age of fifty, leading a charge of the Mousquetaires Gris.

FRENCH MOUNTED MUSKETEER
1660

49
Polish
Winged Hussar
second half of
seventeenth century

A participant in the Battle at Vienna (1683) witnessed the charge of 3,000 Polish winged hussars down the slopes of Kalenberg against the Turkish army, and described it thus: 'The hussars attacked the Godless Turks like angels from heaven'. He was alluding to the wings fixed to the backs of the hussars' armour. The charge, which broke Turkish resistance, partly explains the wings' function: combined with three-quarter ornamented armour covered with bear, leopard and tiger skins, made of eagle, swan, and wild goose feathers, worn by men wielding long lances with multicoloured pennants on the tip, these appendages impressed and intimidated the enemy. Many observers wrote that they were the most beautiful riders in the world: the metal, skins, flags and noble and fiery horses must have been an awe-inspiring sight.

Many drawings, prints and written sources from the sixteenth century depict or describe winged horsemen. According to one source, this habit of ornamentation came from Asia, and was adopted by peoples who became part of the Turkish Empire. Another locates it in medieval Serbia. Besides their ornamental function, the wings had a ritual one – giving the rider 'the ease and speed of a bird carried by the wind', and, supposedly, a protective function too. The nomadic peoples of the Asian and Russian steppes used lassoes to snare horses, and these could also be used for capturing the riders. The wings were supposed to hinder the use of a lasso.

The winged horsemen are most often identified with seventeenth-century hussars because for nearly one hundred years Polish cavalry dominated the spaces of north-eastern Europe. Under their motto: 'First we defeat the enemy, then we count them', they vanquished the Swedes at Kokenhaussen (1601), the Russians at Kushino (1610), the Cossacks at Beresteczko (1651), and the Turks at Chocim in 1621 and 1673, Kamienec Podloski (1653), Vienna and Parkany (1683). These battles, and winged hussars, were not forgotten.

The hussar's breast armour, made on the basis of the Italian anima armour, could withstand a musket shot from 20 paces, while the back armour was impervious to a pistol shot from point-blank range. The most frequent gilt ornaments on the breastplate were the Virgin Mary on the left side and the cross on the right. Besides a heavy lance 5 m/16 ft long, the hussars had a type of combat sabre (*karabela boyova*), a straight sword 170 cm/70 in long for piercing mail coif (*konzerz*) and two pistols carried in saddle holsters.

The hussar units (*coragiew*) consisted of up to 150 men, who were either recruited on the territorial principle or were owned by a Polish magnate: Radziwill, Sobiesky, Potocki, Sienawsky, Lubomirski, Pac, and so on. Each unit had a distinctive pennant for recognition on the battlefield, and each man was attended during campaigns by one or two servants. As the hussars always carried everything necessary for at least two months, each man had one (or more) baggage wagon in the supply train.

POLISH WINGED HUSSAR
second half of seventeenth century

50
Polish Pancerni
seventeenth century

The end of the Thirty Years War, dubbed the 'first world war' by many historians, also marked the end of a long period where weapons' manufacturers competed with makers of armour. Firearms now prevailed over armour in land warfare, and the rivalry was not to be renewed until the coming of the first tanks in 1917.

However, in the east, the development of protection for riders lagged a century behind western Europe. In the second half of the seventeenth century, mail-clad horsemen whose equipment had not changed in a thousand years cruised the expanses of Russia, Poland, the Ukraine, Hungary and the Turkish territories. There were several reasons why this type of protective equipment was retained in the east but abandoned in the west.

In 1600, the workshops of Graz still produced mail short shirts, aprons, collars and sleeves as protection for the parts of the body left vulnerable by a suit of armour. However, a pair of sleeves cost 10 guilders and a shirt 25, while a complete suit of armour was only 6.5 guilders. Armour offered much better protection, and the technology of forging was more advanced and cheaper than the welding or riveting of small iron rings. Because of its high price and the insufficient protection it offered, mail was abandoned in the west at the beginning of the seventeenth century.

In the east things were quite different. Every village blacksmith knew how to cut iron rings and turn them into mail armour. The cost of this labour was much lower, as no special qualifications, complicated tools or furnaces were needed for working plates. Until almost the end of the nineteenth century, mail shirts were produced in Afghanistan and Iran, and worn practically as a national costume.

In western armies, the ratio of infantry to cavalry was about three to one. In the east, it was the other way around: the horseman was still the backbone of the army, and his main weapons were the spear, sabre, long thrusting sword for piercing mail, and the composite bow. Against these weapons mail and a round shield offered adequate protection.

In Poland, the mail-clad riders were called *pancerni* (from the German *panzer* – armour). At the reviews held before the Battle of Vienna (1683), 8,874 pancerni rode past under 84 flags; this was more than half Poland's total cavalrymen at that time. They were heavy cavalry, organized in units of about 100, and the men serving in them belonged mainly to the middle and lower nobility. They were armed with a 3 m/10 ft spear (*rohatyna*), a sabre (*szabla*), a long straight sword (*konzerz*) up to 170 cm/70 in long usually worn on the left side of the saddle, a sabre (*karabela*), a composite bow and a round shield (*kalkan*). Part of the pancerni who fought at Vienna also had a pair of pistols in ornamented saddle holsters.

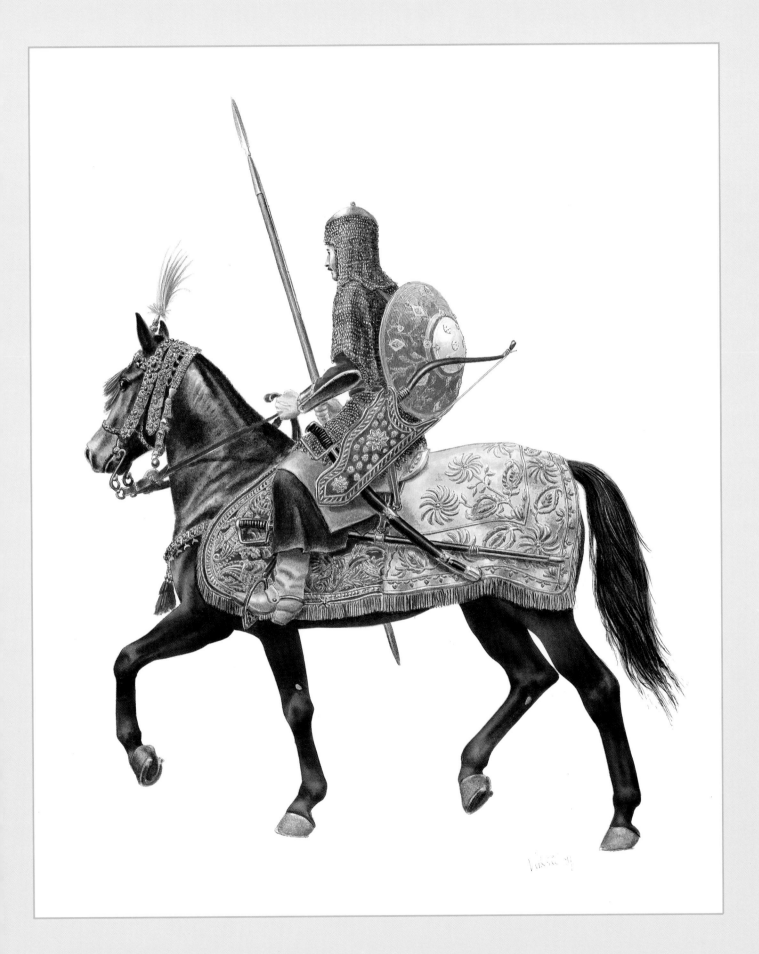

POLISH PANCERNI
seventeenth century

51
Master of the Horse

c. 1660

In the early fourth century, the Athenian Xenophon wrote two books devoted to the art of horsemanship, *Hippike* and *Hipparchikos*. Many of the precepts he offered are still valid today: a rider should gain a horse's confidence, training should be based on rewards and not on punishment, and so on. It was not until a thousand years after Xenophon that stirrups came to Europe from Asia Minor and the art of riding could advance in several directions, including cross-country and hawking, where fast riding and the ability to overcome obstacles were required, as well as skills needed for warfare and tournaments.

In the Middle Ages, or Charlemagne's Age of Chivalry, knights rode long-leg, with their feet pushed forward, and used reins with curb bits and their legs to control their mounts. Riders in the east preferred a forward seat, and rode light horses with a loose rein.

An interest in horses and horsemanship surfaced again in northern Italy in the fifteenth century. Leonardo da Vinci published *The Proportions of a Horse*, in which its measurements were first expressed in 'hands'. In 1550, Frederico Grisone published *Ordine di Cavalcare*, a work patterned upon Xenophon's, in which he also advocated the use of heavy curb bits. This book soon became popular, and on the orders of Queen Elizabeth his work was translated into English. Grisone's influence contributed to the founding of the famous Neapolitan School of Riding and later the Spanish School of Riding, which in 1572 was moved to Vienna, where it still is today.

Grisone was replaced at the head of the Riding School in Naples by Giovanni Baptista Pignatelli, whose best disciples became masters at the courts of Louis XIII and Louis XIV in France and James I in England. The best known was Antoine de Pluvinel, who published *L'Instruction du Roy* in 1623, in which he pleaded for patience and gentleness when working with horses, and recommended saddles adapted to the anatomy of the animal so as not to harm it.

One of the illustrious students of the Naples School was William Cavendish, Duke of Newcastle (1592–1676). While in exile in Antwerp in 1657, he published *La Methode et Invention Nouvelle de Dresser les Chevaux*, illustrated by Abraham van Diepenbeke. Upon restoration of the monarchy, he returned to England and headed the riding school at Bolsover Castle. He believed that a horse executed its rider's commands out of fear more than respect, and would learn everything expected of it by constant repetition. His best-known students were King Charles II and Prince Rupert.

The Duke of Newcastle is also credited with the invention of the double bridle. One (the curb bit) presses on the horse's tongue, preventing it from lifting its head and running; the second (the snaffle bit) presses on the edges of the lips, and a slight action is enough to turn the horse's head to right or left, giving the rider control of the direction of movement.

At the end of the seventeenth and beginning of the eighteenth century, many riding schools opened throughout Europe.

MASTER OF THE HORSE

c. 1660

52
Turkish
Faris Bajrektar
end of seventeenth century

Local Muslims were recruited into mercenary units (*dzema'at* – Arabic for gathering) in the border areas of the Ottoman Empire towards Austria and Hungary. These units (*faris*) numbered between 20 and 50 men; their task was to protect the border and make up the numbers in the operational army in case of war. Dzema'ats were organized territorially in fortresses and townships in the smaller administrative units (*nahys*) and one or more were commanded by an *agha*. A smaller unit (*oda*) was commanded by an *odabasa*. In 1701, in the Gradacac dzema'at on the Austrian border, the commander, Bairam-agha, had 48 men at his disposal: his deputy (*cehay*), the ensign (*bajrektar*), quartermaster (*gulaguz*), scribe (*kyatib*), four officers (*odabasas*) and 40 riders (*farisis*). Their daily pay was: agha 40 *akchy*, cehay 20, bajrektar 15, gulaguz and kyatib 13, odabasa 12 and faris 11.

In war, several dzema'ats, with 500–1,000 men, made up a higher unit (*alay*) commanded by an *alaybey*. The bey was the lowest-ranking officer in the Ottoman army permitted to wear one horse-tail (*tug*); a bey of beys (*beylerbey*) was allowed two, a vizier three, and the sultan had four tugs.

In the Asian steppes, nomads first tied horse-tails to their lances for signal purposes, transmitting messages as far as the eye could see. As this was a means of issuing orders in war, the horse-tail became associated with those who gave the orders – commanders and chieftains. If there were several tugs in the field, they had to be recognized, and their importance assessed. The more horse-tails, the more important the man issuing the order and therefore the order itself. In time, the tug became a war flag, which the Turks brought into central Asia and on their conquests. In the seventeenth century, they were partially replaced by standards in the regular army, but semi-regular and irregular light cavalry units went on using them until the end of the nineteenth century.

The picture shows a faris bajrektar in parade uniform from about the time of the Turkish Siege of Vienna (1683). Muslim craftsmen responsible for the traditionally ornate decoration of warriors' equipment and armament could not use representations of people and animals, but achieved perfection in geometric and floral motifs. Turkish riding equipment – saddles, sabres and shields – were especially valued in Hungary, Poland and Russia, and despite wars and a papal ban, trade with the Muslim craftsmen continued.

TURKISH FARIS BAJREKTAR
end of seventeenth century

53
French
Line Trooper
1690

During the rule of Louis XIII (1610–43), Cardinal Richelieu was chief minister, and was thus the man most responsible for involving France in the Thirty Years War. As part of his reforms, he had unified military administration in the Ministry of War, and battlefield successes were largely due to his reorganization and equipping of the army.

The first French regular units were formed at the beginning of the seventeenth century, from the paramilitary Compagnies d'Ordonnance, formed in the fifteenth century. The first seven cavalry regiments were established in 1635; by 1659, their number had grown to 112. Around 1668, their number levelled out at about 80. The first three on the army list were the so-called 'staff' regiments: Colonel-General, Mestre-de-Camp-General and Commissaire-General. The term 'colonel', derived from the Italian *colonna*, was first used at the beginning of the sixteenth century in Italy, to designate a cavalry unit which fought in column formation. The names of the three staff regiments represent ranks in its staff. The colonel was the commander, the mestre was in charge of the organization of camping and the everyday life of the unit, and the commissaire's responsibility was the securing of provisions in the field and the recruitment of new soldiers. In time, these units were divided into smaller ones, and each officer led one of the companies, so there were colonel's, lieutenant-colonel's, major's and captain's companies. By extension, if 30 regiments of cavalry are treated as a large unit, the first regiment has the honorary name of Colonel-General, the second Mestre-de-Camp-General and the third Commissaire-General. The same principle was applied to dragoon units, so the first dragoon regiment was called the Colonel-General de Dragons, and so forth.

The next ten regiments on the army list, numbers 3 to 13, were called royal regiments from 1672: 4th – Royal, 5th – du Roi, 6th – Royal Etrangers, 7th – Cuirassiers du Roi, 8th – Royal Cravattes, 9th – Royal Rousillon, 10th – Royal Piémont, 11th – Royal Allemand, 12th – Royal Carabiniers and 13th – Royal Pologne. According to the rules of 1690, the royal regiments and those of various princes were allowed to wear blue coats with red cuffs, while the others had grey coats. Only the guard units (Maison du Roi) could wear red coats.

The regiments had two squadrons of two companies each; the companies' complement was 50 men. Until the end of the seventeenth century, regiments were purely administrative formations, created for the unified supply and training of their squadrons and companies. Only at the beginning of the eighteenth century did the regiment also become a tactical battlefield formation.

FRENCH LINE TROOPER
1690

54
Officer, Royal British Dragoons
1685

The administrator of Scotland, George Monck, captured London on 8 February 1660, facilitating the restoration of the monarchy and the accession of Charles II (1660–85). While Charles was living in exile in the Low Countries, the gentlemen of his court formed a horse guard. At the same time the king's brother, the Duke of York, formed his own troop of horse guards, and the king was accompanied by these two units when he returned to England.

The king dissolved the existing army, and formed a regiment of Life Guards from 600 gentlemen of his retinue. From the men of the regiment of horse commanded by General Crook he formed the Royal Horse Guards. The third regiment, created in 1661, was the Tangier Horse.

Catherine of Braganza brought Tangier as her dowry when she married Charles, and he raised a troop of horse numbering 109 men to serve in Tangier. After a parade on St George's Field, they embarked for Tangier, but after evacuation of the Tangier garrison in 1683, the troop returned to England. Two more were added to it, and they constituted the King's Own Royal Regiment of Dragoons. Some years earlier, a dragoon regiment had been founded in Scotland, but it did not cross the border until the death of Charles II. Until the rule of James II, these were the only dragoon troops in the British Isles.

During the 1670s, breastplates, which had been in common use in all line cavalry units in Britain, fell into disuse. They were not officially used again until 1707 in the Low Countries, by cavalry commanded by the Duke of Marlborough, and then only the regiments of horse. The Royal Dragoons were also called the Tangier Cuirassiers, perhaps because breastplates and helmets available after the disbanding of the protector's army were loaded on to the same ship as the Tangier Horse, or perhaps as a tribute to their service as the only regular English cavalry in Morocco. There are several portraits of cavalry (and infantry) officers in the 1680s where the subjects are shown wearing breastplates. At that time breastplates in portraits were considered a symbol of manliness, so they cannot be taken at face value, though it is possible that officers wore breastplates at parades and reviews. The illustration of the Royal Dragoons officer is based on a contemporary painting. In 1751, the regiment's name was changed to 1st Royal Dragoons.

OFFICER, ROYAL BRITISH DRAGOONS
1685

55
Austrian Hussar
1688

In 1526, the Hungarian army were defeated by the Turks at the Battle of Mohacs. The king and the cream of the nobility died in this battle, and Hungary broke up into three parts: one was occupied by Turks, who installed their administration; another acknowledged the rule of Vienna, hoping to gain protection from the Turks; the third proclaimed its own king and converted to Protestantism, so that feudal lords could take over the church's rich lands. These divisions led to constant conflict over the next 300 years: part of the Hungarian nobility acknowledged the rule of the Habsburgs, part fought against them alongside the Turks, and part with the Habsburgs against the Turks. Alliances depended on circumstances and estimates of where the greater evil lurked.

In the Turkish Great March on Vienna (1683), Austria was devastated by Tartars, Akinjis and Hungarian light horsemen – the hussars. They were led by Imre Thököly, a Hungarian lord who headed the uprising against the Habsburgs. With the help of allied forces from Poland and the German statelets, the Austrians succeeded in defending Vienna and then undertook an offensive against Turkey. In 1686, the Austrian army was reorganized and the same year Budim fell to Austrian forces. Preparing for further thrusts east, Austrian Emperor Leopold I founded the first regular Austrian hussar regiment.

The Austrian army had seasonal units of light horsemen which could number up to 3,000 men. These were led by Hungarian and Croatian noblemen, who could change allegiance overnight, especially if the Viennese court tried to make them pay their feudal obligations. Leopold ordered Count Adam Czobor to select 1,000 men and form an imperial hussar regiment which would be paid from the imperial treasury, and be loyal to the crown. It was to consist of men aged 24 to 35, and have horses between 14 and 15 hands tall and 5 to 7 years old. On its formation, the regiment had a staff and ten companies of 100 hussars each. The officers of other Austrian regular cavalry units did not have a high opinion of the hussars, considering them 'little better than bandits on horse'. However, they were very effective in war, and a second regiment under the command of Colonel Deák was formed in 1696; a third, commanded by Colonel Forgach, in 1702.

The year 1688 is taken as the date of the first regular hussar regiment. At slightly earlier dates, occasional regular companies of hussars, consisting of Hungarian emigrants opposed to the Habsburgs, could be found at European courts. However, regular hussar regiments were not founded until 1692 in France and 1695 in Spain.

AUSTRIAN HUSSAR
1688

56
Iranian Lancer
eighteenth century

At about the time of the War of the Austrian Succession and the Seven Years War, in the area now spread over parts of Iraq, Iran, Afghanistan, Pakistan, the southern republics of the former Soviet Union and the north of India, cavalry armies could be found several times the size of those cruising the battlefields of Europe.

During the rule of Shah Hussain (1694–1722), the Glizay Afghan tribe rebelled in Kandahar against Persian rule and declared its independence. Mir Mahmoud, the Afghan leader, captured Kerman and Isfahan in 1722, overthrew Hussain, and proclaimed himself emperor of Persia, but his state soon fell apart. Using the weakness of Persia, Turkey captured parts of western Iran, and Russia took the western and southern shores of the Caspian Sea. The new Persian ruler, the capable and energetic Nadir Shah (1736–47), put the state in order and raised a disciplined army, consisting for the most part of cavalry. In a single thrust, he defeated first Turkey, then Russia, which left him free to deal with Afghanistan, whence a new threat was looming. In 1738, he launched a large military campaign from Isfahan, in which his army, over several years, covered 6,000 km/3,700 miles in constant battles and skirmishes. He captured Basra at the north of the Persian Gulf, Kerman on the Iranian plateau, Kandahar, entered Afghanistan and took Kabul. He went on to capture Lahore and Delhi, down the Ind valley to the Arabian Sea, then north, again by way of Kandahar, through Turkestan, and captured Buhara and Hiva.

On this huge campaign the Persian army consisted of mounted nobility, most of them members of the *quizilbashes* religious-military order, light nomadic cavalry, infantry and artillery. From the end of the seventeenth century, Persian infantry and artillery units had firearms and had been trained by European instructors. The tactics and equipment of the cavalry, however, had remained decidedly obsolescent, with only the quality and beauty of the armour, mail and sabres reaching their pinnacle in the eighteenth century. The basic weapons of upper-class Persians were the light lance, composite bow and sabre. They often carried a mace and short steel javelins in a case. The *chair aina* (four mirrors) armour was so named because it consisted of four plates: breastplate, backplate, and one under each arm, and it was worn over a fine mail shirt. Also part of the protective equipment was a helmet (*sisak*), traditionally ornamented with bird feathers, a round shield with four bosses, and a right-hand guard (*majsur*).

It is interesting that soldiers of the Grande Armée, in Napoleon's march on Moscow in 1812, encountered horsemen from the southern border regions of Russia who wore mail shirts and armour of the type used in Persia several centuries earlier.

IRANIAN LANCER
eighteenth century

57
Mounted Grenadier
1705

Grenadiers were members of chosen, well-armed and well-equipped units of temporary or permanent complement, charged with carrying out difficult tasks. At the time of formation, the men were armed with several hand grenades (*grenade*). They had special uniforms and markings, and were often favoured over other units. These disappeared, but the name was kept for tradition's sake.

Grenadiers first appeared in France during the Thirty Years War, as part of musketeer units. In each unit, several of the bravest soldiers were chosen to attack enemy fortifications in small groups, using grenades. From 1667, each company had four grenadiers – soldiers armed with a sabre, axe and three or four grenades carried in a bag slung over the shoulder. In 1671, a flintlock musket was added to their armament, and a regimental grenadier company, 35 men strong, was formed from those previously dispersed in individual companies. When the battalion was introduced as a formation unit, it also included a grenadier company. Other armies followed and formed grenadier units.

They differed from other infantry units in their headgear, which got its shape primarily for practical reasons: to light the bomb fuse before throwing it, the grenadier needed both hands, and to have both hands free, he had to sling his rifle on to his back. A wide-brimmed hat or a tricorn would have been too big, because the head had to slide between the rifle and its strap, so it was replaced by the more practical cap or colpack. In time, these caps became more elaborate and taller, and in England, Sweden, Russia, Denmark, Prussia and the northern German states the cap came to resemble a bishop's mitre, with an engraved frontplate. In Austria, France, Bavaria and Piedmont the colpack remained in use. A badge depicting a bomb with lit fuse was almost universally adopted as their insignia by European grenadiers.

As musketeers mounted on horses became dragoons, so the grenadiers became mounted or horse grenadiers. In the beginning they were banded into the same regiment as the dragoons, but at the start of the eighteenth century they were organized into separate squadrons and regiments. In England and France these formed part of the guard, while in Russia, Spain, Hanover and Saxony they were line units. In Austria, grenadier companies from dragoon regiments were used temporarily for special assignments, and until the mid-eighteenth century, mounted grenadiers were treated as dragoons – like mounted infantry. Later, they became elite units of heavy cavalry, but retained their name. At the beginning of the nineteenth century, during the Napoleonic Wars, they disappeared from army lists, and only one regiment with this name remained in the French guard.

MOUNTED GRENADIER
1705

58
Bavarian
Prince Philip
Carabinier
1704

To make the arquebus more accurate, the Viennese gunsmith Caspar Zoller devised in 1498 a method of cutting four straight grooves into its barrel. This ensured a more stable trajectory for the ball, and therefore greater accuracy. It also made possible the shortening of the barrel, so that the weapon was lighter and less cumbersome. The French called this an *arme carabiné* (rifled weapon). Also towards the end of the fifteenth century, Arab horsemen called carabins were armed with similar weapons. Their name supposedly came from the Arabic *karab* (weapon), also the possible source of the Turkish *karabul* (marksman).

Whatever the origin of the word, the new weapon was named the carbine, and was issued to troops for whom the arquebus or the musket would have been impractical because of their weight or length; in combat, it was used for targets at close range. As it was a muzzle-loading weapon, carbines which required greater loading speed were manufactured with smooth barrels, and although the main reason for the name – rifled barrel – was thus eliminated, the name stuck. In time, carbine came to be used for shortened versions of infantry muskets or rifles, whether rifled or not.

In 1679, Louis XIV (1643–1715) ordered carbines to be issued to the two best marksmen in each cavalry troop of his line regiments. After the superior effectiveness of horsemen armed with long-range carbines (whose main targets were enemy officers) to those armed with pistols had been demonstrated, Louis decided, in 1693, to form a whole regiment and honoured it with the name of Royal Carabiniers.

Bavarian Elector Maximilian II Emanuel, who had good political and family connections with the French court, formed a squadron of carabiniers in 1696, and the term 'carabiniers' became customary in the Bavarian army.

In the War of Spanish Succession (1701–14) Bavaria joined Louis XIV, but the Franco-Bavarian army was routed in 1704 at Blenheim. The Bavarians retreated across the Rhine and because of heavy losses, the elector disbanded his three dragoon regiments (considered light cavalry at the time), and used part of their manpower to bring three cuirassier regiments up to strength. The remainder (344 men) formed a regiment of light cavalry, with six troops, which he named in honour of his six-year-old son: the Prince Philip Carabiniers.

As fate would have it, in their first campaign, during the battle of Elixem (1705), the Prince Philip Carabiniers bore the full brunt of the British attack led by Wyndham's Horse, also known as 'Carabiniers'. There were heavy casualties on both sides, and the Bavarians lost their troop standard to the British. It was recaptured in a counter-attack by the Arco Cuirassiers from Cologne, and returned to the Bavarians.

Because of a weak inflow of recruits, the regiment was disbanded in 1711, and its men used to supplement others.

BAVARIAN PRINCE PHILIP CARABINIER
1704

59
Swedish Trabant
1709

After the end of the Thirty Years War, in which the Swedish army, led by King Gustavus Adolphus and the commanders Baner, Hurn and Tosterson, scored a series of victories over the imperial armies, Sweden's role in continental affairs was restricted to the Baltic area. In 1675, Charles XI ascended the throne of Sweden, and instituted a series of significant military reforms.

At the end of the seventeenth century Sweden had 2.5 million inhabitants, barely 5 per cent of whom lived in the cities. Its most important rival, Russia, had ten times as many people, and therefore much vaster resources for recruiting its army. Keeping a large number of men constantly under arms would disrupt the Swedish economy, so Charles introduced an administrative organization, the *indelningsverkt*, under which soldiers and officers of the regular army had the right to work the royal land on which farms were allocated to them. There were type projects for the construction of the farms, depending on the rank of the owner. The men from one county belonged to the same unit, so they knew each other, and morale was higher; however, if a unit suffered severe losses, a county could be devastated.

The basic organization of a regiment was four squadrons of 125 men. In peacetime, the troopers worked the land and took part in occasional exercises. In wartime, the regiment's full force would converge at the gathering point and march off to the main army camp, where they underwent continuous training.

At the time of Charles XI, uniforms modelled on French ones of the period of Louis XIV were introduced. Cavalry was divided into national horse and dragoon regiments, with one squadron of Trabant Garde (Royal Yeomanry Guards) and a corps of nobles (*adelsfanan*). In 1685, a royal decree specified a special test for the blades of cavalry swords: they were bent in both directions, and the flat was struck hard against a pinewood plank. The blade was stamped only if it passed this test.

In 1697, Charles XII became king of Sweden. He continued the military reforms, and turned the cavalry into a powerful fighting force, which proved itself in many battles against the Danes, Saxons, Poles and Russians during the Great Northern War (1700–21). How dangerous these battles were is illustrated by the Royal Yeomanry Guards; of 147 troopers who went to war in 1700, only 14 returned in 1716.

SWEDISH TRABANT
1709

60
Russian Dragoon
1709

The accession of Peter the Great (1682–1725) to the throne of Russia marked a turning point in its history. At the beginning of his rule, he realized that Russia could not become a strong country economically unless it had access to the sea. His first aim was a foothold on the Black Sea coast, which meant war with Turkey, and the first clashes showed that the Russian army was not up to Peter's nationalistic ambitions. He therefore reorganized it, modelling it largely on the west European armies, especially in matters of recruitment, administration, armaments and training. In 1689 he ruthlessly crushed an uprising by the Streltzi regulars, and disbanded their units. In 1699, the order was issued for the creation of a new Russian standing army, and eligible men aged between 17 and 32 were recruited for life-long military service. Twenty-seven infantry and two dragoon regiments were created.

The Russian army was traditionally cavalry-oriented; the reason why Peter recruited only two regular dragoon regiments was that he was counting on the numerous yeomanry militia (*dvoriani*) who reported for war with their own horses, armament and equipment, and formed cavalry units. However, after the serious defeat by the Swedes at Narva in 1700, Peter gave up the concept of irregular units and during his rule raised 32 dragoon regiments.

The first were called Schneewanz and Goltz, after their colonels. After 1708, regiments were named for their places of formation and recruitment. They were organized according to the infantry model, in 10 companies of 120 men. Every regiment also had three three-pound cannon. In 1704, an additional company of 140 grenadiers was added to the dragoon regiments; in 1711, these were organized in three regiments of mounted grenadiers.

Until the mid-eighteenth century, Russian cavalry rules envisaged units dismounting and fighting in infantry squares; this was a throwback to the dragoons' infantry training. The reason for this was that Russia lacked large numbers of heavy horses, which were later bought from Germany for the forming of cuirassier regiments.

During the Great Northern War (1700–21), Peter introduced two large dragoon formations: one under General Menschikov, consisting of 11 regiments, the other under General Golitzin, 10 regiments strong. The king thus had at his disposal large corps of mounted infantry armed with artillery and all that was needed for independent action in Russia's vast expanses.

Reputedly, in a conversation between Charles XII of Sweden and Peter the Great, Charles enumerated the virtues of his army, its many successes and captured standards. Peter retorted that Russia was a large country, and that his dragoons could sleep in their saddles. It is a fact that the Russian dragoons and their horses were tough, and that they suffered remarkably small losses from exhaustion, illness or cold during military operations and long marches.

RUSSIAN DRAGOON
1709

61
English
Guard Trooper
beginning of eighteenth
century

King Charles II returned to London in 1660, disbanded the existing army and created a new one. From 600 gentlemen who had followed him in exile, he formed three troops of the senior regiment of the Life Guard. The first troop was called His Majesty's Own Troop of Guards, the second after the king's brother (later to become James II) His Royal Highness the Duke of York his Troop of Guards, and the third His Grace the Duke of Albemarle his Troop of Guards, in honour of General Monck, who had captured London and made possible the return of the king. After Monck's death in 1670, the third was renamed the Queen's Troop of Guards. From the existing regiment of horse commanded by General Unton Crook, the king formed the regiment of Royal Horse Guards in 1661.

After the introduction of grenadier companies into infantry regiments, the same was done in cavalry units. Grenadiers had the task of carrying out special assignments, and in 1678, a division of mounted grenadiers was added to every troop of the Life Guards; these were called horse grenadiers.

In 1685, James II succeeded Charles II but was deposed three years later in the so-called Bloodless Revolution. During his reign, the English cavalry was the best equipped, best trained and most highly paid regular cavalry force in Europe. Seven regiments of horse were formed during his rule; five in 1685: Queen's Regiment of Horse (later 1st King's Dragoon Guards); Earl of Peterborough's Regiment of Horse (2nd Dragoon Guards – Queen's Bays); Earl of Plymouth's Regiment of Horse (3rd Prince of Wales's Dragoon Guards); Earl of Thanet's Regiment of Horse (4th Royal Irish Dragoon Guards), and the Queen Dowager's Regiment of Horse (6th Dragoon Guards – Carabiniers). The Earl of Shrewsbury's Regiment of Horse (5th Princess Charlotte of Wales's Dragoon Guards) was founded in 1686, and the Earl of Devonshire's Regiment of Horse (7th The Princess Royal's Dragoon Guards) in 1688.

In 1746, for reasons of economy, the 3rd and 4th troops of horse guards in each regiment were disbanded, and the first three regiments were converted into (cheaper) dragoons, with the courtesy name of Dragoon Guards. It was only towards the end of the eighteenth century that the Dragoon Guards became a kind of elite, compared to ordinary dragoons.

British Household Cavalry regiments were rarely used in foreign wars. During the Seven Years War (1756–63), the Royal Regiment of Horse Guards fought alongside three guards regiments at the Battle of Warburg (1760). However, household and guard units were not fully utilized until the Napoleonic Wars. In 1813, at the Battle of Vitoria, the Household Brigade, made up of 1st and 2nd Life Guards and the Royal Horse Guards, took part; at Waterloo in 1815, the 1st King's Dragoon Guards were added. In this engagement, the brigade, commanded by Lord Somerset, disposed of 1,200 sabres.

ENGLISH GUARD TROOPER
beginning of eighteenth century

62
Cuirassier
1710

An interesting test was recently conducted in Austria with original firearms from museum collections, manufactured between 1571 and 1700. A target the shape and height of an average human figure was shot at from 30 m/100 ft and 100 m/330 ft. About 20 smooth-bore arquebuses, matchlock and wheel-lock muskets were tested, and the results showed that the probability of a hit at 100 m/330 ft from a weapon fastened to the test table was 40 to 50 per cent; at 30 m/100 ft, the ball could pierce armour 3–4 mm thick, and at 100 m/330 ft armour 1–2 mm thick (for comparison, a modern Belgian FN assault rifle can pierce 12 mm of armour at 100 m/330 ft). The only real difference among the weapons was that the later models were lighter and had a greater rate of fire. Three pistols were also tested, one made in 1620 and the other two in 1700. The probability of scoring a hit from them at 30 m/100 ft (also fastened to the test table) was much higher: 85 to 95 per cent. All three could pierce 2 mm of armour.

The firepower of infantry and cavalry forced armoured riders from the battlefields towards the end of the seventeenth century. The rate of fire was also increased, while the cost of firearms manufacture went steadily down. For a while, armoured cavalry tried to fight back with the use of musket-proof breastplates and pistol-proof backplates; together, these weighed over 15 kg/33 lb, and the protection provided did not justify its high price or inconvenience. At the beginning of the eighteenth century, France, Bavaria, Austria, Saxony, Brandenburg, Denmark and Holland equipped their cuirassiers with breastplates and backplates which were similar, and with hats under which steel skull-caps were worn. In 1698, Britain officially abolished the use of armour in regiments of horse, but reintroduced a breastplate worn under the coat in 1707, at the time of the War of the Austrian Succession. Armour was not seen again until the coronation of George IV (1821), and then only for the Household Cavalry.

The weight of a breastplate was about 5 kg/11 lb, and it was about 2–3 mm thick. It was primarily meant to protect the rider from cutting and thrusting weapons, although it was effective against firearms too, up to a certain distance. Until the mid-eighteenth century, armour was made up by the forging of hot metal plates on specially shaped casts. The first series of breastplates made by cold pressing was manufactured in Prussia in 1755. This new technology made possible the production of larger batches of armour of standard quality.

CUIRASSIER
1710

63
Saxon Dragoon Drummer
1735

Drums have been used since pre-biblical times. On the battlefield, they assisted commanders in the issuing of orders, in raising the morale of their troops and in frightening the enemy.

At the end of the seventeenth and beginning of the eighteenth centuries, units were increasingly fighting in rigid line formations, and soldiers were trained to move and fight according to precisely determined rules. At the wings and rear of infantry battalions were several drummers who determined the speed of movement by the rhythm of their playing. One beat equalled one step, and the rhythms used were march, normal pace, quick pace, double pace, charge, and so on.

When some foot soldiers became mounted troops (dragoons), their drummers also went on horseback. Their role remained the same: following the dragoons into action when they fought dismounted. The drummers were the last to mount and first to dismount, waiting for a certain signal from their officers.

Saxon dragoon regiments, like many others in Europe, had a staff and six companies of 95 men each. The staff had one drummer, and each company two. The drum-major, a member of the staff, conducted the band of company drummers, who marched at the head of the regiment on ceremonial occasions.

The 8th Austrian Dragoon Regiment (formed as the Dampierre Regiment in 1619) had a rare privilege: its men had once saved the life of Emperor Ferdinand II, so it was allowed to play its drums while passing the imperial palace.

The elite regiments of heavy cavalry also had drummers, but only for ceremonial purposes – reviews and parades. Dragoon drummers had infantry drums, slung on a strap over their shoulders, while those of cavalry regiments used kettle drums fastened to their horses' saddles. They were not supposed to be taken off the saddles and, richly ornamented with coats-of-arms or regimental badges, in time they reached large proportions, up to 1 m/3 ft in diameter. The kettle drummers formed part of the regimental orchestras, and rode white or dappled horses, just like the trumpeters. In time, as dragoon regiments acquired more characteristics of real cavalry units, their infantry drums were replaced with kettle drums.

At the beginning of the eighteenth century Hungarian hussar regiments had a drummer. These regiments were owned by Hungarian magnates who raised them and outfitted them for war. The traditional drummer had the role of messenger, who, according to custom, called the populace to city and village squares and read them orders and proclamations. The hussar drummers called the men to the regimental flag. In the second half of the eighteenth century, when these regiments lost their seasonal character and moved into barracks, drummers were no longer needed.

SAXON DRAGOON DRUMMER
1735

64
French Gendarme
c. 1750

The French mounted knight or nobleman, fully armoured, armed with a lance and riding on an armoured horse, was called a *gendarme*, derived from *hommes d'armes*, equivalent to the English man-at-arms. Towards the end of the fifteenth and at the beginning of the sixteenth century, French cavalry had 15 Compagnies d'Ordonnance, each 100 'lances' strong. A lance in this sense represented one gendarme and two less well-armoured horsemen riding unarmoured horses, called *chevaux-legers*. All together they were called the Gendarmerie. In the mid-sixteenth century, the chevaux-legers, whose main role was support in combat, replaced their lances with firearms.

The French army consisted of the Gendarmerie – about 5,000 men in all – and the Guard, which represented the cream of the armed forces; the king also had at his disposal personal companies, with the primary task of protecting the sovereign in war and peace. The first of these, consisting of 100 Scottish infantrymen, was formed in 1442 by Charles VII (1422–61); his successors had several and, in the middle of the sixteenth century, they numbered about 600 men. Other members of the royal family also had the right to personal bodyguard companies not exceeding 150 men in strength.

In 1665, all these were reorganized into 17 companies of regular cavalry, 250–300 men strong. Pursuant to the earlier tradition, some were called Gendarmerie de France, and the others Chevaux-legers. The first four (including the 1st Scottish and 2nd English) belonged to the king; the rest to the queen and various princes. Each company was commanded by a captain-lieutenant, equal in rank to a colonel in the other line regiments of cavalry. A cornet ranked as a lieutenant-colonel, a sergeant as captain and a brigadier as lieutenant. Four gendarmes shared a servant, who took care of them and transported their equipment on a pack horse.

The Gendarmerie did not belong to the Guard, but had practically the same status. On the battlefield, they were kept as a cavalry reserve numbering 2–3,000 men, usually together with the Guard, and intervened at critical moments, charging regardless of casualties. They took part in all the French campaigns, with notable success, but by the time of the Seven Years War, there were only 10 companies of gendarmes.

Like the Guard, they were allowed to wear red coats; breastplates could be worn underneath. Each company had its own insignia, embroidered with silver thread on the men's pistol holders, saddle-cloths and carbine belts. They were armed with a rifled carbine, two pistols and a sword, and wore a steel skull-cap (*calotte de fer*) under their hats.

FRENCH GENDARME
c. 1750

65
Prussian Cuirassier
1756

When Frederick II ascended the throne of Prussia in 1740, he had at his disposal 22,544 horsemen, half of them in 12 cuirassier regiments. Immediately after his coronation, he formed a squadron of Garde du Corps cuirassiers (after 1756 they were a cuirassier regiment of three squadrons, number 13 on the army list). He also changed the name of the 10th Cuirassiers to Gendarmes, the 11th to Leib-Karabiniers, and the 3rd to Leib-Kuirassiers, and incorporated them all into his Guard. The other regiments had black breastplates, but the Garde du Corps had shiny metal cuirasses.

At the beginning of the War of the Austrian Succession, at the Battle of Mollwitz in 1741, Frederick learned of his victory only when in flight. The Austrian cavalry had broken their Prussian opponents and nearly captured the Prussian king, but his excellent infantry turned defeat into victory. As Frederick wrote afterwards, he had the opportunity of seeing on the battlefield how bad the cavalry was that he had inherited from his father. Most officers were not up to their jobs, the men were afraid of the horses, hardly anybody could ride well, and training was carried out on foot, like infantry. Worst was their lack of speed. He decided to reorganize them, and issued numerous rules and instructions, which had most effect in the cuirassier regiments, which became the best of their time in Europe.

Frederick decreed that recruits for the cuirassier regiments had to be healthy and strong, not less than 160 cm/5 ft 3 in in height, so that they could carry the heavy equipment. Those chosen were the best recruits of the regimental areas, mostly peasants' sons who knew their way around horses. A minimum height of 157 cm/61 in was decreed for the horses, and the most sought after were the Holstein breed. Holstein horses were bred in monasteries in the valley of the Elbe from the thirteenth century, local mares being crossed with Neapolitan, Spanish and oriental stallions. The first licensing regulations were issued in 1719, and in 1735, the first state stud farms in Prussia began to breed Holstein horses for the army. These were very popular, and were exported to many European countries. They were large, black and dark brown, strongly built and dynamic in motion.

After 1735, Prussian cuirassiers replaced their buff coats with tan-coloured ones of stout cloth. Towards the end of that century, the uniforms of Prussian and other European cuirassiers changed to white; the colour was the only reminder that they had once been made of leather. Cuirassiers were armed with a carbine, two pistols and a broadsword (*pallasch*), and regiments were of five squadrons, each about 150 men.

At the Battle of Rossbach, in 1757, five cuirassier regiments, with a total of 23 squadrons, under the command of Major-General Seydlitz, twice charged the French troops and those of the German statelets (*kreis*), and decided the outcome in favour of Prussia.

PRUSSIAN CUIRASSIER
1756

66
Prussian
Bosniak Lancer
1760

In what was, until recently, Yugoslavia there was a republic, now a state, called Bosnia which occupies the same place as a medieval state of that name. Its inhabitants of the Muslim faith are called Bosniaks. They were originally Christians who converted to Islam after Bosnia came under Turkish rule, at the end of the fifteenth and beginning of the sixteenth century, to preserve their holdings and privileges. In feudal Turkey, anyone who owned land had the obligation of military service in case of war, so Bosniaks were found in all Turkish armies of that time.

In 1740, the War of the Austrian Succession began. Prussian King Frederick wanted to annex the rich province of Silesia, but Austria opposed this, which was deemed sufficient cause for war. In the early part of the war, known as the First Silesian War, Saxony was on the side of Prussia, but decided to switch allegiance. In preparation for a possible continuation of the war, military emissaries were sent to the Ukraine in 1744 to recruit men for the Saxon cavalry. The response of the Cossacks was disappointing, but Saxony managed to lure from the Turkish army about 100 Bosniaks – light horsemen armed with lances, who were guarding the Turkish border in the Ukraine. The Bosniaks left for Dresden.

On their arrival, Prussian emissaries in Saxony offered the Bosniaks more, so they marched off again, from Saxony to Prussia. In 1745, Frederick founded a regular Bosniaken Korps, one troop in strength, which became part of the 5th Hussars, also known as the Black Hussars (Totenkopf), their symbol being a death's head.

Hostilities continued as the Second Silesian War, and ended in 1748, but the Bosniaks remained in service. In the same area, and for similar reasons, another war soon started. In 1756, Prussia occupied Saxony, triggering the Seven Years War. The magnitude of operations and insufficient Prussian human resources forced Frederick to recruit soldiers outside his borders. Light horsemen from the east – Poles, Lithuanians, Tartars and Muslims – were incorporated into the Bosniak units, which, by 1760, had grown to 10 squadrons. That same year, the Bosniaks became a regular light cavalry regiment, number 9 on the army list.

After the end of the war in 1763 the regiment was disbanded, only one squadron being kept for ceremonial purposes. In 1778, another war broke out between Prussia and Austria, this time over Bavaria. The Bosniaken Korps was again filled out to 10 squadrons, mainly with recruits from the Ukraine and Poland. In this war, which had no major battles, the Bosniaks suffered heavy losses in surprise attacks by the Austrian hussars.

Towards the end of the eighteenth century, Poland disappeared from the map of Europe: one part was annexed by Russia, another by Austria and a third by Prussia. Prussia recruited 15 squadrons of light horsemen from its part of Poland; but these troops were Bosniaks in name only. As Poles made up the majority, the units were renamed the Korps Towarczys in 1799. After the Prussian defeat by Napoleon in 1806, the Towarczys were disbanded.

PRUSSIAN BOSNIAK LANCER
1760

67
Swedish Hussar
1761

Sweden came into frequent conflicts with Russia over control of the Baltic in the seventeenth and eighteenth centuries. However, at the time of the Seven Years War, the dominant political forces in Sweden were in favour of peace with Russia, which was decisive in their opting to join the alliance against Prussia. Swedish military experts decided that their army could not conduct serious operations without light cavalry support, especially against an enemy with ten regiments of hussars.

Accordingly, in December 1757 the government signed a contract with Captain Count Frederik Putbuss and Lieutenant Philip Julius Bernhard von Platen obliging them each to raise a corps of two 100-men hussar squadrons. The following year another contract was signed, this time with Major Baron Georg Gustaf Wrangel, for recruiting a ten-squadron hussar regiment, with a total of 1,000 men. It was formed in Rügen, then in one of the Swedish Baltic provinces, and named the Kungliga Husarregementet (Royal Hussar Regiment). As it had been formed in a German-speaking province, the language of official communication and command was German. Lacking their own rules and regulations, the Swedish hussars were trained according to the Prussian drill-book.

The famous Prussian marshal of the Napoleonic Wars, Count Blücher (1742–1819), served for a time in the Swedish hussars. Fifteen-year-old Blücher was at his brother-in-law's in Rügen, and when the Swedish hussars were sent off to Pomerania, somehow young *junker* Blücher was one of them. As fate would have it, he was captured in 1760 by the Prussian 8. Belling hussars, who enlisted him in their ranks. After 49 years of service, Blücher led the 8th Hussars at the Battle of Jena in 1806.

In 1761, Sweden decided that one hussar regiment was not enough, and another was formed. The existing regiment was divided into two, each six squadrons strong, and their manpower made up to 800 each. The new regiment, commanded by Colonel Putbuss, had blue uniforms and were known as the Blue Hussars, while Wrangel's men were known as the Yellow Hussars; blue and yellow being, of course, the Swedish national colours. Another mandatory part of the uniform was the moustache; for beardless hussars such as Blücher, false moustaches were provided.

SWEDISH HUSSAR
1761

68
Tarleton's
Light Dragoon
1780

Until 1745, British cavalry consisted only of horse and dragoon units; by the standards of the time, these belonged to the heavy and medium cavalry respectively. During the Jacobite rebellion, the Duke of Kingston organized at his own expense a regiment of light horse, modelled on the hussar regiments. It was disbanded the following year, but the Duke of Cumberland, using practically the same men, formed a regiment of light dragoons. After valuable service in Flanders, that was disbanded in 1748. In 1755, it was decided that three regiments of dragoon guards and eight dragoon regiments were to have a troop of light dragoons, consisting of three officers and 65 men. After the Seven Years War, they too were no more.

In 1759, Colonel George Augustus Eliott raised a whole regiment, the 15th Light Dragoons, made up of six troops, and numbering 400 men. In the Battle of Emsdorf, the Light Dragoons charged three times through enemy lines, and captured a whole battalion of French infantry, at the cost of 125 men and 168 horses. This heroism was later emblazoned on their helmets and colours. Five more regiments were formed, so the name became commonplace in the British army, but unlike other cavalry units, they had special equestrian training and practice in shooting from the saddle. The horses they used were smaller than those of other units – 15 hands, three inches (154 cm/60.5 in).

At the beginning of the American War of Independence (1775–83) a unit of American loyalists with a core of British troops was formed: the British Legion, under the command of Lieutenant-Colonel Banastre Tarleton. Part of its cavalry was recruited from the 16th and 17th Light Dragoons, the only two British cavalry units to serve in America during the war. These men were called Tarleton's Light Dragoons, and were organized and outfitted to British standards.

The war developed as a series of minor clashes and conflicts between small units in a relatively large space. Cavalry, even though few in number, were extremely valuable in skirmishes, reconnaissance and ambushes, akin to the hussars' role in Europe. In May 1780, Tarleton and his dragoons covered 170 km/105 miles in 54 hours and in a surprise attack at Waxhaws, near the North Carolina border, destroyed several companies of Colonel Buford's infantry, who were hurrying to relieve the siege of Charleston. Tarleton also inflicted great losses on the forces of General Gates at Camden and General Sumter at Fishing Creek, which brought him the name of 'Bloody Tarleton'. However, he suffered a catastrophic defeat at Cowpense, and never recovered.

After the end of the war, the dragoons brought back their distinctive helmet, designed by Tarleton himself. It was officially accepted as part of the British Light Dragoons' equipment, and remained in use until the end of the nineteenth century.

TARLETON'S LIGHT DRAGOON
1780

69
American Continental Dragoon
1778

Taking advantage of the new numerical superiority of its settlers and the strength of its colonies, Britain pushed France and Holland out of America. However, the 13 British colonies, growing economically more powerful, began demanding increased independence, dissatisfied with being simply a source of raw material and a market for finished products. At the beginning of 1775, there were open clashes between the colonists and the British regular army, and these signalled the beginning of the American War of Independence.

Towards the end of 1776, when war operations were well underway, George Washington wrote to Congress: 'From the Experience I have in this Campaign of the Utility of Horse, I am Convinced there is no carrying on the War without them, and I would therefore recommend the Establishment of one or more Corps.' Congress promptly approved the outfitting of 3,000 light horsemen, but this was easier said than done. During the war, the strength of the American regular cavalry never topped 1,000, and it was seldom indeed that several hundred were gathered in one place.

At the beginning of 1777, four regiments of continental light dragoons were formed from provincial militias and volunteer units: Blend's Virginia Light Horse became the 1st Dragoons; Colonel Elisha Sheldon raised the 2nd regiment, Sheldon's Dragoons; the 3rd and 4th were also named for their founders (Baylor's and Moylan's Dragoons). American light dragoons resembled their British counterparts in organization and equipment. Every regiment had six troops, whose hypothetical complement was 280 men; in practice, this number never surpassed 150.

The jockey helmet, decorated with a tail and strengthened with a brass comb, became standard issue not only for the dragoons, but for militia units as well. Lacking standard equipment and armament, every man came to the gathering point with what armaments he had, so that the arsenal included even Indian spears and tomahawks. The 2nd Dragoons, for example, armed themselves with 149 broadswords discarded by the Brunswick Prinz Ludwig Dragoons after their defeat at Bennington in 1777.

Eighty troopers of the 4th (Moylan's) Dragoons and 45 of McCall's Mounted Militia, commanded by Colonel William Washington, distinguished themselves at the Battle of Cowpense, in 1781, when they routed Tarleton's 200 green-uniformed dragoons of the British Legion and 50 troopers of the 17th British Light Dragoons, and forced the demoralized British infantry to lay down their arms.

AMERICAN CONTINENTAL DRAGOON
1778

70
Prussian
Porzellan Dragoon
1806

With the agreement of the German Emperor, Duke Frederick of Brandenburg crowned himself king of eastern Prussia, under the title of Frederick III (1713–40). Two large territories were thus united into the one state, Prussia, which gradually spread in all directions, by marriage inheritance and buying. Stretching from the Niemen to the Rhine, in a series of larger or smaller territories which did not border each other, it was a state neither ethnically nor geographically homogeneous. A strong army was its basis, and one of the strongest factors in its cohesion. The Prussian king invested most of his income in the army, which soon became the fourth largest in Europe.

A strange exchange was agreed during a meeting in 1717 between Duke August II of Saxony and Frederick. To replenish his depleted military treasury, August consented to take a collection of priceless Prussian porcelain, giving in exchange a cavalry regiment of 600 men. The regiment marched off to Prussia, where it became the 6th Dragoon Regiment, known among the people as the Porzellan Regiment.

In 1744, Prussia had 12 dragoon regiments, which remained unchanged until 1802, when an additional two regiments were founded. The 5th and 6th regiments differed in that they had ten squadrons each, while the others had five. In 1806, they had complements of 1,682 men, which made them the strongest cavalry regiments in the Napoleonic Wars, and each squadron had 12 trained marksmen armed with rifled carbines. Their tasks included reconnaissance, patrolling, protection of troop movements and obstruction of enemy skirmishers.

Before the war with France in 1806, the Prussian cavalry had very high standards of equipment, training and horses: dragoon regiments had outstanding horses of the Holstein, Trakehner and Ostfriese breeds. Regimental officers were punished if their horses or equipment were not in good shape, so, generally speaking, great attention was accorded them. Dragoon regiments were equal in rank, status and training to cuirassier regiments of the line. Prussian cavalry had morale and fighting spirit as in the time of Frederick the Great, so it represented a significant obstacle for the French, as Napoleon warned in a special bulletin before the beginning of the campaign.

At the time of the decisive Battles of Jena and Auerstedt, the 6th Dragoons, under the command of Colonel Johann Kasimir von Auer, were in eastern Prussia, as part of the corps of Marshal L'Estocq, and thus avoided destruction and disbanding. After minor skirmishes with the French at Tuchel and Sorquitten, they marched off to Russia with the rest of L'Estocq's forces. In 1807, they took part in the bloody and indecisive battle at Eylau, fought in a snowstorm. After the peace of Tilsit, most of the Prussian army was disbanded.

The 6th Dragoons preserved four of their squadrons; after the Treaty of Paris, in 1808, these became the nucleus of the Neumark Dragoon Regiment.

PRUSSIAN PORZELLAN DRAGOON
1806

71
Polish National Cavalryman
1794

Opposing the creation of a capitalist, bourgeois society, and fearing that events would develop as they had in the French Revolution, in 1792 the Polish Catholic church and the feudal magnates called upon Russia, Austria and Prussia to intervene in Poland. The weak Polish army could not stand up to the superior enemy troops, and the king himself contributed to the general treason by ordering them to surrender. Poland was occupied, and nearly half of its territory was annexed by Russia and Prussia. This state of affairs could not last for long, and in 1794 there was an uprising under the leadership of Tadeusz Kościuszko. At first the national army was successful, inflicting several defeats on the enemy, the severest being that of the Russians at Raclawice. However, the insurrection was put down by the end of the year.

The bases of the Polish army were the national infantry and cavalry. In 1792, the royal army had 17,500 infantry and 17,600 cavalry organized in light regiments (*lekkiej kawalerii*). This unusual ratio between infantry and cavalry troops was a reminder of the glorious past of Poland's mounted forces. The Polish cavalry, the pride of the army, was organized in people's brigades (*brygada kawalerii narodowej*). Two belonged to the Wielkopolski, Ukrainski and Malopolski counties, and one to Litewski county. Each consisted of two regiments with three or four squadrons, and its full complement was between 1,200 and 1,800 men. Besides the people's brigades, there were the so-called royal regiments, one of guards – the Gwardia Konna Koronny, with 487 men, and six Pulki Przedniej Strazy Koronny, of about 1,000 men each. A regiment of lancers, the Pulk 5 Ulanow, had 390 men.

During the 1794 uprising, all the regiments became part of the people's army, with their old organization and names but barely half of their manpower. A large number of volunteer cavalry regiments and independent squadrons were formed, usually numbering between 100 and 700 men. Besides national names, they were also called after their colonels, for example, Gorzynski (620 men), Zakarzewski (600), Moskorzewski (640), Kwasniewski (300), Dabrowski (522), and so on. Major Krasicki formed a hussar regiment of 203 men; in all, the cavalry numbered about 20,000.

Red and dark blue were the dominant colours in Polish cavalry uniforms, characterized by the national jacket (*kurtka*) and the *czapka* cap, later the model for the uhlan czapka adopted by nearly all European armies. The czapka has roots in the ancient past. The oldest drawings date from 1560 and 1565, showing respectively the caps of a professor and a Cracow merchant. Polish emigrés in the army of General Dabrowski, which fought as part of the French army in Italy in 1796–1800, arrived dressed in uniforms which soon became officially accepted in the French army.

POLISH NATIONAL CAVALRYMAN
1794

72
Russian Chevaliers-Gardes Trumpeter
1800

Modern Russia began with the reign of Peter the Great (1689–1725). Using both wisdom and violence, he initiated the reforms which, inside 50 years, converted a medieval state into a European power. Securing his power was one of the key factors in Peter's design for vanquishing the old and traditional structures in Russia; the other was the army, which he reformed. He disbanded the traditional *streltzi* infantry units, and engaged the services of many veteran German, French and Scottish officers, who were familiar with modern military thinking. The Russian army was then organized on the model used by many western armies.

Peter's tour of European courts in 1697, and the large number of foreign officers in his army – one of them, Scotsman Patrick Gordon, attained the rank of general – led Peter to base his court also on the European model. He was a man who learned from experience: in the struggle for the throne, he had nearly been killed by the palace guards, so he chose 71 of the more distinguished noblemen from his dragoon regiments and formed a royal bodyguard called the Kavalergvardia. Ordinary troopers in this unit held the rank of captain, corporals were lieutenant-colonels, and so on, so the usual complement was: one captain (Peter), one captain-lieutenant (field marshal), one lieutenant (lieutenant-general), one sergeant (colonel), three corporals (lieutenant-colonels) and 60 troopers (captains). After the accession of Catherine the Great (1762–96) the Kavalergvardia was renamed the Corps des Chevaliers-Gardes.

The map of Europe began changing during the French Revolutionary Wars (1792–1800). Napoleon Bonaparte, at the head of the French expedition to Egypt in 1798, seized Malta from the Order of St John. Looking for an ally, Volhynian Prory of the Maltese Order offered the grand mastership to Emperor Paul I of Russia (1796–1801), who accepted, and declared war on Napoleon.

In 1799, Paul, fearing for his life (not unreasonably, as two rulers before him had been murdered), disbanded the existing squadron of Chevaliers-Gardes, and formed his own bodyguard under the same name, with one general, two colonels, five officers, nine NCOs, one trumpeter and 75 troopers. As grand master of the Maltese Order, he decreed that his Gardes should wear the Maltese Cross on their breasts and backs, while retaining the *chipyer* star with the two-headed eagle on the saddle-cloths. In 1800, two more squadrons were added to the palace contingent, and they were designated senior regiment of guard cuirassiers. Each squadron of the Regiment des Chevaliers-Gardes had a standard of the vexillum type, in shape and name similar to those of the Roman legions. They were of rose-pink brocade, with a white cross and a silver fringe.

In 1805, the complement of the Chevaliers-Gardes was increased to five squadrons and 875 men. The same year, at Austerlitz, their charge routed a French infantry battalion, but they suffered serious losses in a counter-attack by the Grenadiers à Cheval of the imperial guard.

RUSSIAN CHEVALIERS-GARDES TRUMPETER
1800

73
French
Grenadier à Cheval
1807

In 1676, Louis XIV chose the bravest grenadiers from his line infantry regiments and formed a 250-man guard cavalry regiment named the Grenadiers à Cheval de la Garde. Their task, as bravest of the brave, was to spearhead the charges of the infantry or cavalry of the Maison du Roi.

After the end of the French Revolutionary Wars, in which France had resisted all the attacks of the First Coalition and strengthened its army, the first consul, Napoleon Bonaparte (1769–1821), took total power into his hands. Two guard units were formed: the Foot and Mounted Grenadiers of the Consular Guard. They had very similar uniforms, and identical headgear – the distinctive tall black bearskin hats. After Napoleon was crowned emperor in 1804, the mounted regiment was renamed the Grenadiers à Cheval de la Garde Imperiale.

On the day of the renaming, the regiment had 1,018 troopers in four squadrons, with two companies each. Distinction in military service, personal bravery and the recommendation of high-ranking officers were necessary conditions for joining this unit, as was a minimum height of 176 cm/5 ft 9 in. The men were paid 300 francs a year and had the status of an elite. The regiment was mounted on heavy black horses, mostly of the Norman or Anglo-Norman breeds; only the 30 trumpeters rode grey or white horses.

Two events occupy special places in the regimental history. At the Battle of Austerlitz (1805), the Russian cavalry guard led by Grand Duke Constantine, brother of Emperor Alexander I, succeeded in breaking several of the French lead infantry battalions and stopping Napoleon's attack on the centre of the allied formation. The emperor ordered his Grenadiers to counter-attack. The white-coated Russian Chevaliers-Gardes met the French charge, but suffered heavy losses, and Grand Duke Constantine barely escaped with his life.

At the winter Battle of Eylau (1807), a charge against the Russian positions through a raging blizzard led the Grenadiers behind enemy lines. When their commander, Colonel Lepic, appraised the situation, he realized that he had no choice but to reorganize his men and charge back out. The double charge through enemy lines brought Lepic the rank of general, and a prize of 50,000 francs in gold, which he divided among his men.

The Grenadiers took part in all the major battles of the Napoleonic Wars. Three hundred of them were decorated with the Legion of Honour, while all the officers were given the rank of Officers of the Legion of Honour.

FRENCH GRENADIER A CHEVAL
1807

74
Austrian Uhlan
1809

The term uhlan was supposedly derived from the Turkish *oglan*, meaning child (the term infantryman was derived in a similar way from the Italian *infante*). Horsemen armed with spears and sabres were to be found in the forces of the Saljuq Turks in the fourteenth and fifteenth centuries. In the sultan's cavalry guard, 1,000 chosen noblemen were in the Sipahi Oglan unit and in the sixteenth century, light horsemen called uhlans appeared in Poland and Lithuania.

After the partition of Poland among Russia, Prussia and Austria in the eighteenth century, it was in these states that the first regular uhlan regiments organized and dressed according to the Polish model were formed. The first three in Russia, formed in 1805, were called Lithuanian, Tartar and Polish, clearly indicating their origin.

In 1791, Austria engaged the services of several companies of *ulanow* in the border region of Galicia. Joseph II had formed them in 1784 as a squadron of Galizischen Adelsgarde (in Polish *gwardia galicyjska*). One of its members was Joseph Poniatowski, later to become a marshal in Napoleon's army. In 1791, during the reign of Leopold II, the existing divisions were transformed into a regiment of uhlans. According to the Polish model, it had four squadrons, two of them armed with lances (241 cm/95 in shaft, 21 cm/8 in blade), and two with carbines only. The uhlans with carbines were supposed to break the enemy with their gunfire, thus laying the ground for the attack with spears.

The uhlan uniform copied the Polish cap (*czapka*) and jacket (*kurtka*). The horse equipment was the same as for the hussars, but from 1798 the *shabraques* had rounded rear corners. In 1801, the new cap was introduced, with a height of 23 cm/9 in and a square top.

In 1798, the 2nd regiment of uhlans was formed from Degelman's Frei Korps; the 3rd was raised in 1801, and the 4th in 1813. From 1805, uhlan regiments had eight squadrons, each with 150 men, plus 90 dismounted troops in a reserve squadron. Counting staff, it comprised 1,360 men and 1,212 horses. The organization of the regiments was not changed after 1809, but before the war with Napoleon the complement was raised to 1,481 men and 1,414 horses. After the campaign and defeat of 1809, the number of squadrons was decreased to six. In the wake of the Battle of Wagram, Polish troops serving in the French army gathered the lances discarded by Austrian uhlans, foreshadowing the 1810 decision to make this their official weapon. The Austrian army list of 1813 gave the regiments according to the names of their proprietors (*inhabers*): one, Herzog zu Sachsen-Coburg-Saafeld; two, Fürst Schwarzenburg; three, Erzherzog Carl Ludwig, and four Kaiser Franz.

AUSTRIAN UHLAN
1809

75
Brunswick
'Black' Hussar
1809

After the Battles of Jena and Auerstedt in 1806, in which the Prussian marshal and Duke of Brunswick, Karl Wilhelm Friedrich, was killed, and after the fall of Prussia the same year, the duchy of Brunswick was annexed by the French and added to the kingdom of Westphalia, ruled by Napoleon's brother Jerome. Friedrich Wilhelm, the duke's son, went into exile in Austria.

Having been defeated by France in 1805, Austria was preparing to get even, and in 1809, after the uprising against the French occupation troops in Spain and the national awakening in Germany, Austria decided to go to war. Friedrich Wilhelm of Brunswick allied himself with the Austrians, and raised a corps of infantry and cavalry troops. One thousand hussars and the same number of infantry lined up before the duke in the town of Nachod, in Bohemia. Because of the tragedy that had befallen his family and his country, the duke chose black for the uniforms, and the skull-and-crossbones for the shakos, hence the name Schwarze Schar (Black Band) for this corps. Equipment and weapons were procured from Austrian arsenals, and the hussar regiment had four squadrons and a horse artillery battery of four guns.

The operations of 1809 ended in Austrian defeat and an unfavourable peace settlement. The duke did not accept defeat; he decided to make his way with his troops to the Atlantic coast and sail thence to England. In his way were the troops of Westphalia, and the city of Halberstadt, defended by 3,000 of Jerome's soldiers. By nightfall, the duke's troops had taken the city gates and the remaining 500 men of the hussar regiment, commanded by Major Schrader, burst into the main square of the city under cover of darkness. The enemy reserve of several hundred men located there soon surrendered, and, except for pockets of resistance Halberstadt was captured. After resting and recruiting several hundred men, the duke reached Brunswick in two days. However, numerous pursuers were after him, and messengers had been sent to alert the garrisons still on his way. In a week, and after several small skirmishes, the Black Band of 1,600 men had made its way to Elsfleth, on the west bank of the Wasser. By various ruses, the hussars led their pursuers away from the place of embarkation, so they had time to sell their horses before they left. The duke and his men boarded British ships and, after disembarking at Yarmouth and Grimsby, entered British service. The following year, they took part in the expedition to Spain, together with British, Italian and Spanish troops under the command of Sir John Murray.

The hussars remained in British service until mid-1815. However, for the Hundred Days campaign, in which Napoleon was finally defeated, the duke raised another regiment of Black Hussars numbering 730 men, so for a short time there were two regiments serving under the same name.

BRUNSWICK 'BLACK' HUSSAR
1809

76
Hanover Dragoon
1809

Hanover is a county (*Landkreis*) and the capital city of the province of Lower Saxony. In the Middle Ages, it was part of Saxony, and after its division in 1180 it became part of the duchy of Brunswick-Lineburg. In 1692, German Emperor Leopold I gave Ernst August the title of elective duke, and until 1814 Hanover remained an electoral duchy. In 1714 the current duke's son, Georg Ludwig, became King of England as George I, and Hanover entered into a personal union with Great Britain which lasted from 1714 to 1837. In 1794, during the Revolutionary Wars, Hanover provided Great Britain with an auxiliary corps of 18,000 men for operations in the Netherlands. After seven months of Prussian occupation in 1801–2, it raised an army of 16,000 men which Napoleon disbanded when he occupied Hanover in 1803.

A group of patriotic officers, supported by the Duke of Cambridge, recruited volunteers to go to Great Britain and join the fight against Napoleon. These became the King's German Legion (KGL). By 1806, the corps had grown to two regiments of heavy dragoons, three regiments of light dragoons, ten battalions of infantry and six batteries of cannon. It was equipped and organized according to the British model.

The Legion's heavy cavalry consisted of two regiments, the first commanded by Colonel Georg von Bock and the 2nd by Major-General Otto von Schulte. Both had uniforms similar to the British dragoons, but the 1st with dark blue and the 2nd with black facings.

In 1809, Great Britain sent troops commanded by the Duke of Wellington to Spain; these included the King's German Legion. At the Battle of Salamanca (1812), both regiments of dragoons were brigaded, under the command of von Bock. The French, commanded by Marshal Marmont, lost the battle, and began to retreat. General Foy's infantry division, deployed in squares, was protecting the retreat. Von Bock attacked the French squares with his heavy brigade, the 1st Dragoons striking first. The close salvo fired by the disciplined French troops mowed down nearly the whole first line of the Hanoverians, and the remaining dragoons were stopped by a wall of bayonets. One of the wounded horses fell on the French infantrymen, and for a moment opened a breach in the square, through which the dragoons of the second line rushed, and, the battalion of 500 men soon surrendered. Encouraged by this success, the men of the 2nd Dragoons attacked the next square, and the demoralized French laid down their arms without a fight, but the attack on the third square was beaten back with heavy losses. The dragoons lost 127 men and twice as many horses.

The attack by von Bock's brigade was one of the rare instances in the Napoleonic Wars of a cavalry charge succeeding in breaking an infantry square.

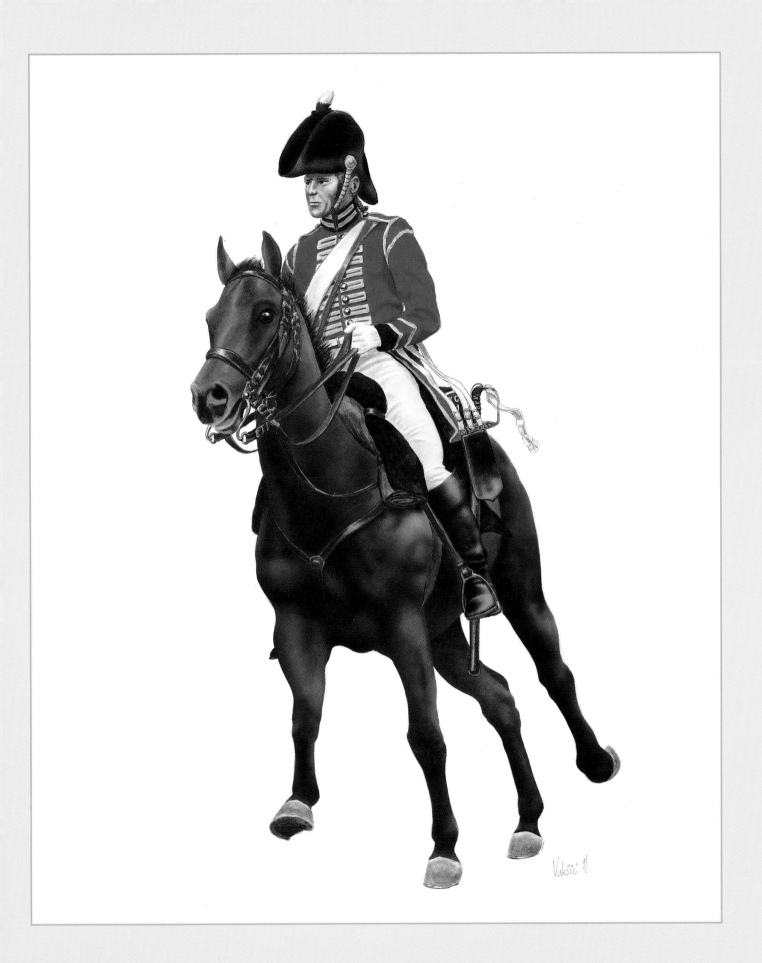

HANOVER DRAGOON
1809

77
Saxon
Garde du Corps
1812

In the war against Napoleon in 1806, Saxony was allied with Prussia, but after the defeat at Jena it abandoned the Prussian cause and cast its lot with the other German statelets under the French protectorate in the Confederation of the Rhine. The elector of Saxony, Friedrich August (1750–1826), who had been given the title of king and the crown of the grand duchy of Warsaw by Napoleon, put at the service of his benefactor a force of 20,000 excellent soldiers. In 1810, the army of Saxony had been reorganized on the French model, and after the introduction of general conscription it had increased to 31,000 men.

Like all the other members of the Confederation of the Rhine, Saxony took part in Napoleon's Russian campaign of 1812. Commanded by General-Leutnant von Thielmann, and forming part of the French and Allied cavalry, a heavy brigade of cuirassiers, consisting of the Garde du Corps and Von Zastrov regiments, crossed the Russian border with four squadrons each. Many experts consider this was the finest heavy cavalry brigade of the Napoleonic Wars. At the Battle of Borodino, the Saxons charged the key Russian position of Raevsky redoubt, and were the first inside it, making possible its capture, but they lost nearly half their 850 men. Napoleon, who was following the action from his command post, was told that the buff-coated Saxon horsemen had been the first to enter the redoubt, but showed little sense of fairness, saying he could see only the blue coats of the French cuirassiers. However, General Latour-Mabourg commented that they had not needed cuirassier armour to justify their reputation (an allusion to the fact that their armour had been left behind in Warsaw).

Only 20 officers and 7 men of other ranks returned from the Russian campaign, and 48 prisoners of war were released later. Both regimental standards were lost, as were the famed silver trumpets of the Garde du Corps. During the autumn operations of 1813, the Saxon troops were still on Napoleon's side, unlike the other members of the Confederation of the Rhine, which had crossed over to the Allies. After the Battle of Leipzig, so did the Saxons.

The name Garde du Corps, taken from the French army of Louis XIV, was first used in Saxony in 1710, when a regiment of that name was founded. After the death of August II and the weakening of Saxony, it was disbanded, but as a token of his alliance with Prussia and an acknowledgement of the Prussian Garde du Corps, Friedrich August raised a regiment of the same name in 1804, which became the senior unit in the army. It was mounted on black horses of the heavy German breeds, although there is evidence that the officers rode on grey horses. The regiment's trumpeters used silver trumpets, and were dressed in gala red uniforms. After the reorganization of 1810, uniforms were patterned on the French, but the regimental lace and facing colour were kept.

SAXON GARDE DU CORPS
1812

78
Colonel of French 7th Hussars
1813

After the French Revolution of 1789, the new republican government raised 13 hussar regiments between 1791 and 1795. In twenty years of war, all these regiments had more or less similar fates, but the 7th Hussars were rather different.

The regiment was founded in 1792, in Compiègne, by Convention Decree, as the Hussards de Lamothe. Next year, the name was changed to 7me Régiment de Hussards, and in 1794 they became part of the army of General Pichegru, fighting against the Anglo-Dutch forces of the so-called First Coalition.

That year cold weather came very early, and military operations were suspended, the troops retiring to winter quarters. The English forces returned to England. At the beginning of November, the Waal river, which separated the two armies, froze over. The French commander received news of possible revolution in Amsterdam; he did not hesitate, but gathered his forces and crossed the Waal over the ice. The race against time was on; the enemy had to be prevented from organizing resistance in Holland. Light units had the most work, and especially the light cavalry which was in advance of all the other troops. In the night of 11 January 1795, the 7th Hussars arrived at the Dutch fleet's anchorage at Texel, and saw the fleet frozen in its moorings. The hussars rode over the ice and surrounded the ships, forcing them to surrender, and became the only cavalry regiment to make naval history.

In the war with Prussia, in 1806, the 7th were brigaded with the 5th Hussars; the 935 men were placed under the command of General Lasalle, the most popular and 'most hussar' of all the French generals of the Napoleonic Wars. Lasalle's motto was that one could not be a good hussar after the age of thirty; he proved it, in a fashion, by dying at the head of his division at the age of 34.

Pursuing the Prussians, he and his hussars covered 1,150 km/715 miles in 25 days, or 50 km/30 miles a day on average. Finally, at the head of 500 men, he captured the fortress of Stettin, with 6,000 men and 160 cannon. This success brought his men the name of Brigade Infernale, and Lasalle command of a light cavalry division.

After the Russian campaign of 1807, the famous portrait of Lasalle in the uniform of the 7th Hussars, with general's markings on his sleeves, was painted; this was the same uniform in which he was killed at Wagram in 1809.

After the restoration of the First Empire in 1815, the 7th Hussars became the senior regiment in the hussar army of the Colonel-General de Hussards, which gave the right to various privileges. When they were finally disbanded towards the end of the same year, due homage was paid to this distinguished unit.

COLONEL OF FRENCH 7TH HUSSARS
1813

79
Nizza Cavalryman
1848

One of the decisions of the Congress of Vienna (1815) was the creation of the kingdom of Sardinia (Piedmont), which also encompassed the former republic of Genoa. The House of Savoy soon lost independence and became Austrian vassals, and the desire for freedom put Piedmont at the forefront of the struggle for Italian unification. From 1848 to 1866, with short intervals of peace, there were three wars against Austria, from which the small states of northern Italy emerged free and united.

The revolution in France in 1830 gave great hopes to the Italian patriots of the Risorgimento. In Piedmont, a restructuring of the army resulted in great improvements in the quality of training, especially in the cavalry, and the organization, armament and uniforms of the cavalry were regulated by the rule-book of 1833. In 1835, six cavalry regiments were converted into two brigades: the 1st, consisting of the Nizza, Savoia and Novara Cavalleria, and the 2nd, consisting of the guard Piemonte Reale, Genoa and Aosta cavalry. The next year, the same six regiments were grouped into three brigades, and in 1841, each had six squadrons, one of which was armed with lances. The peacetime formation had 825 men and 633 horses, in wartime there were 1,128 men and 959 horses.

The beginning of the nineteenth century saw the rise of classicism in French art, which drew its inspiration from Ancient Greece, a free civil society which was also the model for the French Revolution. In the field of military equipment, classicism found distinguished expression in the cavalry helmet, which was a copy of the Ancient Greek model. In 1811, it was issued to French line lancers and carabiniers; in 1815 to the English life guards and Belgian carabiniers; soon after, it was worn by nearly all the heavy cavalry forces of Europe. The Piedmont Rules of 1833 envisaged the use of such a helmet, and it was made in 1840 according to the design of court painter Palagio Palagi, and called the Minerva helmet.

The Nizza cavallieri were armed with heavy cavalry sabre, two pistols, and a very short carbine (*pistolone*). The lancers had a lance with a swallow-tailed pennant, in the Italian national colour – blue.

In 1848, upon hearing of the revolution in Vienna, the inhabitants of Milan rose and ousted the Austrian garrison, and Piedmont immediately declared war on Austria. The campaign lasted a year, and ended in the defeat of the Montagnards. The Nizza cavalry played a prominent role. A certain sergeant Fiora had his horse killed under him, and was surrounded by four Austrian uhlans; he killed one with his lance, wounded another, and chased off the remaining two, running after them. A similar feat was performed by a sergeant Prato, also surrounded by four Austrians, this time hussars; he killed one and chased off the remaining three.

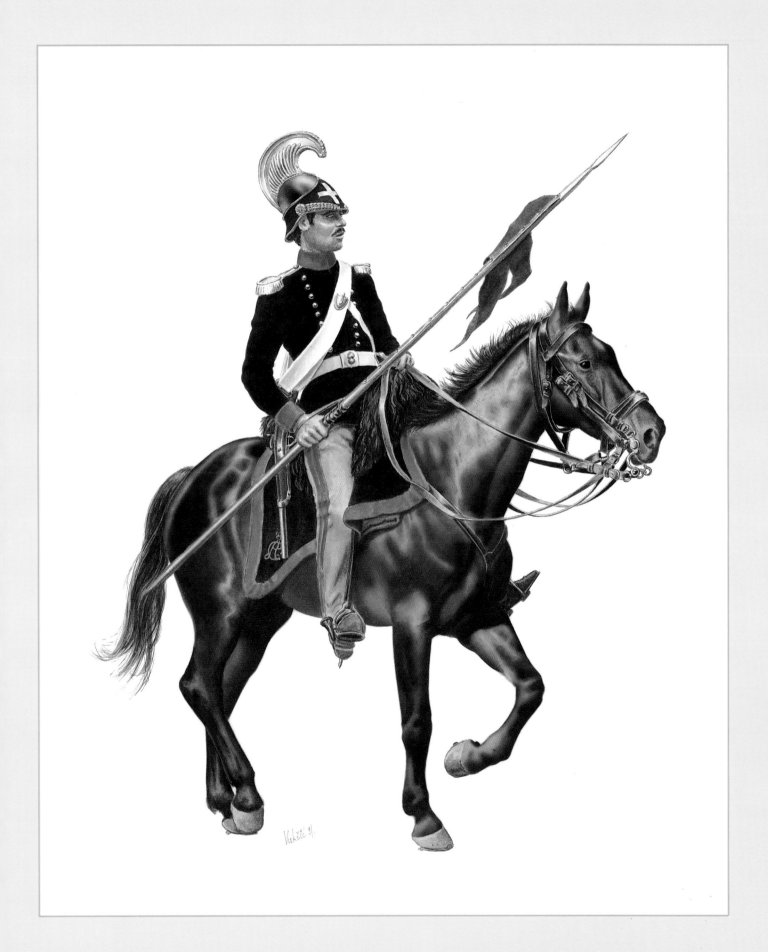

NIZZA CAVALRYMAN
1848

80
Officer of 2nd US Dragoons
1848

In 1821, Mexico obtained freedom from Spanish rule, and the way was open for American trade in New Mexico. Caravans of traders began crossing land controlled by the Comanche tribe, and this quickly led to war. To protect the trade route to Santa Fé and El Paso, the American government formed the US Regiment of Dragoons in 1833. It had ten companies, A to J, and a complement of about 750 dragoons. They were armed with a carbine, two pistols and a heavy cavalry sabre.

On the other side of the continent, there was also trouble. In 1819, the United States had bought Florida from Spain, and the first clashes with the Seminole Indians grew into a prolonged conflict. In 1836, Congress authorized the formation of the 2nd US Regiment of Dragoons. The best marksmen in the regiment were armed with Colt's six-shot revolving rifles. After the end of the Seminole War in 1841, two companies of the 2nd Dragoons stationed in Fort Jesup, Arkansas, were armed with lances, but they were unused to such weapons and slow to adapt, so the experiment was cancelled a year later. The following year, the regiment was to be disbanded, but a compromise was found in its conversion into an infantry rifle regiment. After lengthy discussion, Congress gave the regiment its horses back, and in 1844 it again became the 2nd US Dragoons. Infantry rifles were replaced with Hall's single-shot carbine, model 1843.

The same year that the 2nd US Dragoons were founded, Texas declared its independence, but Mexico still claimed suzerainty. In 1845, the United States annexed Texas, and this caused the Mexican-American War (1846–8).

Before the start of hostilities, President Polk sent General Taylor at the head of the 2nd Dragoons and 3,000 men in an 'observer's mission' to Texas. On 24 April 1846, 1,600 Mexican cavalrymen crossed the border at the Rio Grande, and surprised two companies of the 2nd Dragoons. Eleven Americans were killed and the remaining 52 captured. Taylor told the president that hostilities had started, and crossed the Mexican border. At Palo Alto, a brigade of 800 Mexican lancers attempted to attack Taylor's position from the flank, but were broken by the charge of two companies of the 2nd Dragoons and one of Texas Rangers, armed with Whitneyville-Walker Colt revolvers. Mexican casualties were 257 dead; Taylor lost 55 men.

The clash at Palo Alto demonstrated a new aspect of war: the American riders were far fewer in numbers, but were armed with revolvers and succeeded in defeating the enemy, inflicting great losses in the process. From then on, close combat with revolvers was the preferred mode of fighting of the US cavalry, eclipsing the sabre clash.

OFFICER OF 2ND US DRAGOONS
1848

81
Mexican Lancer
1848

Mexico went to war with America assuming that its more numerous army would prevail, but things did not work out quite as planned. The American cavalry had honed its fighting edge in conflicts with the Indians and was then probably the best-equipped and highest quality mounted troop in the world. Mexico, on the other hand, had inherited traditional Spanish military doctrine, including many French characteristics after Napoleon's occupation in 1808–13. Although the Spaniards had been driven from Mexico in 1829, the army retained units called cuirassiers, hussars, lancers and dragoons.

Rules published in 1837 decreed that regiments should have four squadrons of two companies each. Each company's complement consisted of a captain, a lieutenant, two ensigns, a first sergeant, three second sergeants, nine corporals, two trumpeters, 52 mounted troopers and eight dismounted troopers. In every regiment, the first company of each squadron was armed with lances, a weapon popular in the Mexican cavalry. These lances were made of beech or nut wood, and were 3 m/10 ft long, and their points were in the form of a 20 cm/8 in knife, with three or four cutting edges separated by gutters. The shaft of the lance was 3 cm/1 in thick. As for firearms, pistols and vintage carbines were used. For example, a large number of Tower single-shot, muzzle-loading muskets had been acquired from Britain and, although use of these had been discontinued in Britain in 1838, their production was resumed in Mexico.

Besides the regular regiments, there were 17 regular and 12 independent Presidial Companies of Lancers. The Presidial Companies, 50 to 60 men strong, were permanently posted in the *presidios* (frontier forts). In 1846, on the San Diego road at San Pascual, the California Presidio, 75 men strong, clashed with several companies of the 1st US Dragoons, commanded by Colonel Kearny. The dragoons could not use their firearms, because their gunpowder was wet, so they fought with swords against lances. The dragoons lost three officers and 15 troopers, and as many again wounded, while one lancer was taken prisoner and ten were wounded.

The Mexican command envisaged raising whole series of irregular companies armed with lances in case of war. The tasks of these units were to be reconnaissance, patrol and attacks on enemy lines of communication. In 1843, the Jalisco Lancers was formed. It had two squadrons, and its men were dressed in the Polish mode, with *czapkas* instead of helmets. The Mexicans were born equestrians, and rode high-quality mounts, 15 hands tall, with a lot of Arab and Spanish blood. Horses of this breed are still found today, under the name of Native Mexican.

MEXICAN LANCER
1848

82
Dragoon of Scots Greys
1854

In 1678 the Royal Regiment of Scots Dragoons was raised from two independent Scottish companies of dragoons, and in 1681, the number of companies was increased to six. At a 1694 ceremonial parade in Hyde Park, the regiment rode past the reviewing stand on grey or white horses, and was therefore named the Scots Greys. Both the name and the colour of the horses remained unchanged until the twentieth century.

After the union of England and Scotland in 1707, the official name of the regiment was changed to Royal Regiment of North British Dragoons, and in 1713, Queen Anne conferred to the regiment the second rank of dragoons on the army list. When the bicorn hats of all dragoon regiments were replaced with brass helmets, the Scots Greys were given bearskin caps.

At the Battle of Waterloo (1815), the 2nd Dragoons were brigaded with the 1st Royal and the 6th Inniskilling Dragoons under the command of Major-General Sir William Ponsonby. This brigade, 416 strong, was dubbed the 'Union Brigade', because it consisted of one Scots, one English and one Irish regiment. The Union Brigade charged the French infantry, and Sergeant Ewart captured the standard of the 45th Regiment; however, the charge had led them too far from the Allied positions, so they suffered heavy losses in a counter-attack by the French cavalry. Ponsonby was among those killed.

This charge was immortalized by Lady Butler in her famous canvas. Both cavalry and art experts say that it is symbolical of the cavalry and everything the mounted elite represented in its time. Many French generals and marshals considered the British cavalry the best in Europe, but it was precisely this spirit of the charge and their ardour, illustrated in the painting, which led them out of control, deep behind enemy lines and exacted a high price in human lives. The Union Brigade lost over 200 men in its celebrated charge, depriving Wellington of one-fourth of his cavalry.

Part of the attraction of the painting surely also lies in the appearance of the Scots Greys. Not many heavy cavalry regiments were mounted on white horses in Europe, for several reasons. One was practical: it is hard to keep white horses clean, and their care requires more time than that of dark horses. The selection of white or grey horses would have been an extreme indulgence, but the Scots Greys rode horses of nearly pony size, some 15 hands tall, of which there were plenty in Scotland and Wales, and many came naturally in white or grey.

In the Crimean War, at the Battle of Balaclava (1854), the successful charge of the Scots Greys was overshadowed by the notorious charge of the Light Brigade. It was, in fact, the charge of the Heavy Brigade, commanded by General Scarlett, that decided the battle in favour of the Allies. As it had forty years earlier, the Heavy Brigade could have borne the name of Union, as it consisted of the 1st Regiment of Royal Dragoons, 4th and 5th Regiments of Dragoon Guards, 6th Regiment of Dragoons – Inniskilling and the 2nd Regiment of Dragoons – Scots Greys, and had a total force of about 800 men. Placing 300 (about 200 of them Scots Greys) in the first line and 500 in the second, Scarlett broke a force of some 3,000 Russian cavalry threatening the Allies' flank.

DRAGOON OF SCOTS GREYS
1854

83
Texas Ranger
1861

Ranger was a term originally used for the keepers of the royal woods and hunting grounds; in a similar way, the word is now used for guards of US national parks. At the beginning of the eighteenth century, however, it was used to designate the members of a special rapid-deployment infantry unit for reconnaissance and ambush actions, recruited by Great Britain in North America and Canada. The organizers of the ranger units were James Oglethorpe and John Gorham, but the best-known was Robert Rogers, who recruited 24 men from the Massachusetts militia for the French and Indian War in 1754–5. The following year, His Majesty's Independent Companies of Rangers, or simply Rogers' Rangers, numbered about 700 men.

During the American War of Independence, Thomas Knowlton recruited several companies in Connecticut, and they took part in the Battle of Bunker Hill and the Siege of Boston. After the Battle of Long Island, he formed a whole regiment from new recruits. In the Mexican War (1846–8), Colonel Jack Hay raised the Texas Regiment of Mounted Volunteers, 500 men strong, which fought as part of General Tyler's army in Mexico. Two of the Ranger captains became famous: Ben McCulloch and Samuel Walker.

Every ranger was armed with a rifle and one or two Colt revolvers. The Texas Rangers played a particularly prominent role in Tyler's drive towards Monterey, clearing the road of Mexican guerrillas and preventing enemy reconnaissance and attacks on the American rearguard and communications.

In the first battle of the Civil War (1861–5), at Bull Run in 1861, two volunteer aides of Confederate General Beauregard distinguished themselves: B. Frank Terry, of Bend County, Texas, and Thomas Lubuck, of Houston. Confederate President Jefferson Davis conferred on Terry the rank of colonel, and made Lubuck a lieutenant-colonel with the right to raise a ten-company regiment of rangers in Texas for service in Virginia.

Terry and Lubuck started looking for volunteers, who were supposed to bring their own weapons and equipment, the Confederate government providing them with horses. Each ranger had to be armed with at least a double-barrelled shotgun and one six-shooter revolver. Terry had four Colt revolvers. In less than a month, over one thousand volunteers marched off to Houston, where they became the 8th Texas Cavalry Regiment, better known as Terry's Texas Rangers. Although Colonel Terry was killed in their first major engagement, in December 1861, the regiment kept its name until the end of the war.

TEXAS RANGER
1861

84
Hussar,
1st US Hussars
1864

After Bull Run, which was the first battle of the Civil War, President Abraham Lincoln called half a million volunteers to arms. The Federal government's ambitious plan of equipping and training such a large number began to have results within two years. This mobilization of human and industrial resources (repeated in the First and Second World Wars) was dubbed the American War Machine.

At the beginning of the war, the Union army could count on six regular cavalry regiments; by the end of 1861, there were 82. The following year, the Union had 60,000 troopers, and almost 300,000 horses had been bought for the army. The regiments were organized in cities, counties or loyal states, and were named after them – the 1st New York Cavalry, the 7th Ohio Cavalry, and so on. All Union regiments were simply called cavalry; comparing their tactical role with similar European units, we could safely classify them as dragoons; they had to fight on foot as well as on horseback.

Towards the end of 1863, both sides began to lose momentum, and the war was less attractive to volunteers. In New Jersey, the authorities decided to make recruitment into the cavalry seem more interesting and challenging, and posters with the message 'A Horse to Ride and a Sword to Wield', advertising the 1st US Hussars Regiment, were displayed throughout the state. The chance of being a hussar instead of an ordinary cavalryman soon provided the necessary number of men. The Newark company dressed them in attractive uniforms, similar to the Austrian hussars', while the state spared no expenses for their equipment and armament. At the beginning of 1864, the regiment, completely mounted and equipped, passed through Washington, and as was the custom of the time, President Lincoln reviewed the unit in front of the White House. Its appearance in hussar uniforms drew the attention of the press, and reports appeared in all the dailies. The army list included them as the 3rd New Jersey Volunteer Cavalry Regiment, and the number '3' was sewn within a wreath on their caps. However, they remained the only regiment to be called 'hussars', and, because of their ornate uniforms, were also nicknamed 'The Butterflies'.

The regiment showed that it was made of sterner stuff than butterflies. At Berryville Turnpike, on 13 September 1864, the hussars routed a strong force of Confederate cavalry, and helped to capture the 8th South Carolina Infantry, with their standards and commander. They also took part in the battles at Appomattox, Cedar Creek and Five Forks.

HUSSAR, 1ST US HUSSARS
1864

85
French
Chasseur d'Afrique
1864

After the failure of European expansion, marked by the fall of Napoleon, the French began showing greater interest in Algeria. The immediate pretext for intervention was a petty insult to the French consul by a local dignitary. After a naval blockade of the Algerian coast, a French expeditionary corps under General Bourmont landed in 1830, but when they tried moving inland they encountered fierce resistance from the Algerian tribes.

Preparing for operations in the Algerian hinterland, the French government decided to form regular units of light colonial cavalry which could take on the remarkably mobile desert warriors. Two squadrons of Chasseurs d'Afrique, each about 120 strong, were formed as part of the Zouaves infantry regiment in 1830. They consisted mainly of Frenchmen, with only a few Arabs. Their equipment and weaponry were the same as for metropolitan chasseur units, but their uniforms were better adapted to local conditions. The squadrons were mounted on hardy Arabian horses which bore well the vicissitudes of the stony and sandy deserts. Besides the Chasseurs d'Afrique, several squadrons of Spahis, about 100 strong, were formed from cavalrymen discharged from Ottoman service. The majority of the troopers were Arabs, the officers mostly French.

Algerian rebels led by Abd El-Kader were responsible for seveal serious defeats of the French forces. Warriors mounted on fast horses executed surprise attacks on isolated outposts, inflicted casualties and melted into the mountains and desert. The French military presence increased, the number of soldiers arriving from the metropolis growing constantly. To counter the rebels' guerrilla tactics, by 1839 the French had formed four regiments of Chasseurs d'Afrique, each six squadrons strong, and after a long and exhausting war, Abd El-Kader conceded defeat in 1847.

During the Battle of Balaclava in 1854, the 4th Regiment of Chasseurs d'Afrique attacked the Fedioukine Heights and silenced the Russian cannon, thus facilitating the infamous charge of the Light Brigade, and in 1864, seven squadrons of the 1st, 2nd and 3rd regiments were sent to Mexico as part of the expeditionary corps escorting Archduke Maximilian. They proved remarkably effective, because they were used to similar climatic conditions and guerrilla tactics in North Africa. In their regimental history, the Chasseurs recorded wars on three continents: Africa, Europe and America.

During the Franco-Prussian War (1870–1), they distinguished themselves with an attack on the flank of the Prussian infantry at Sedan. In 1887, two more regiments were formed, and at the beginning of the First World War the number was increased to eight.

FRENCH CHASSEUR D'AFRIQUE
1864

86
Hussar of Austrian Legion, Mexico
1865

After the war with the United States (1846–8), the young liberal bourgeoisie emerged victorious from the political struggles in Mexico. They abolished the privileges of the army and the church, adopted a constitution, and declared void Mexico's foreign debt. The leadership of the Catholic church began an open struggle against the new authorities and President Benito Juárez, and because of unpaid debts, foreign powers intervened in Mexico in 1861.

The combined forces of Great Britain, France and Spain captured the port of Vera Cruz. Another 28,000 French troops soon arrived; commanded by General Bazaine, they crushed the resistance of troops loyal to President Juárez and took Mexico City. Trying to strengthen his position *vis-à-vis* Prussia, Napoleon III installed Austrian Archduke Ferdinand Maximilian of Habsburg as emperor of Mexico (1864–7).

Maximilian was followed to Mexico by an Austro-Belgian expeditionary force of 8,000 men, commanded by Colonel van der Smisien. This force was nominally commanded by Maximilian, but was paid by France, and immediately joined the conflict.

The Austrian contingent numbered 6,545 men, and included a hussar regiment of six squadrons, made up of Hungarian volunteers from the Habsburg Empire. The hussar's uniform differed from the Austrian and more closely resembled its original model – the Hungarian folk costume. They were armed with a rifled single-shot muzzle-loading model 1859 pistol and a sabre. The saddle and the rest of their riding equipment was identical to that used in the Austrian light cavalry. Maximilian was sentimentally fond of his hussars, and nominated one company as the Empress's Own Hussars of the Guard.

In February 1865, the United States government demanded the withdrawal of foreign troops from Mexico, or it would take military action to back Juárez. Napoleon III immediately ordered the withdrawal of French troops. After their withdrawal Maximilian organized his own 'Imperial Army', numbering 25,000 men. Amongst these was a hussar regiment, 1,000 strong, formed from the former Hungarian volunteers and commanded by Colonel Count Karl Kevenhiller. The regiment had scarlet uniforms, which resulted in the name of Red Hussars – the main bulk of Maximilian's cavalry wore green uniforms. They remained loyal to Maximilian until the end; many of them dying in the final fighting around Queretaro. Maximilian surrendered, was tried by the Juaristas, convicted and shot in 1867.

HUSSAR OF AUSTRIAN LEGION, MEXICO
1865

87
Cossack
Trumpeter
end of nineteenth century

In the eighteenth century the power of Russia grew; its territory increased in aggressive wars against Poland, Sweden, Turkey and the Cossacks. In one of many wars, Empress Catherine II (the Great) decided to wipe out the *zaporozhiye* and in 1776, she succeeded. About 5,000 Cossacks fled to Turkey, and the rest found refuge in the villages of Malorussia. In 1783, thanks to the efforts of the zaporozhiye commander, Anton Golovatov, the displaced cossacks were re-formed as a regiment, and became part of the Russian forces as the Army of Faithful Cossacks.

In the Russo-Turkish War (1787–91) the Turkish army crossed the Kuban river in the Caucasus area, but were beaten by weaker Russian forces. The warriors from the zaporozhiye shone in these battles, and were given the name Black Sea Cossack Regiment. After the end of the war, Catherine decided to settle these men in the area around the Kuban river; they were given high decorations and good land, with the obligation of defending the border against the Turks and the Cherkez peoples of the mountains. The first detachment of Black Sea Cossacks – about 4,000 men, headed by Colonel Sava Biyeli – arrived in 51 boats and one large ship, and the next year (1793) the rest came, 17,000 men, women and children.

The Black Sea Cossacks existed as an independent army until 1860, when Kuban province was formed. A series of edicts (*ukazy*) established a new administrative order, with civil and military power in the hands of one man, the administrator of Kuban province and head *ataman* of one of the Cossack regiments. The province was divided into seven regions, each of which raised several hundred Cossacks for peacetime service. The main occupation of the male population, besides horse-breeding, was life-long service in the army. From the moment a Cossack took the oath, at the age of 20, he was considered to be in the employ of the state. For a year he was in training; for four years in the first category of active service, for another four years in the second, for a further four in the third, and his remaining years until the age of 48 were spent in the reserve. A Cossack had to provide his own horse and weapons.

When the Black Sea settlers arrived in the Caucasus, they found a local mountain breed of horses – *kabardin*, known since the sixteenth century. Breeding kabardin mares with Karabakh, Turcoman and Arab studs resulted in an excellent breed of horses, with a medium height of 152 cm/60 in, which was equally well suited to mountains and steppes. This new breed kept the name kabardin, and was characterized by resiliency and surefootedness on the steepest paths. In a test conducted in 1935–6, a group of riders on kabardins covered 3,000 km/1,850 miles in 37 days, under very difficult conditions.

Regular Black Sea units, like all other Muslim cossack regiments, had black uniforms, and near their breast pockets they wore metal or silver bullet cases, richly adorned. The trumpeters wore red so that they could be distinguished from the fighting troops. It was considered a disgrace to fire upon non-fighting soldiers like trumpeters.

COSSACK TRUMPETER
end of nineteenth century

88
Prussian Cuirassier
1871

In the Prussian army, cuirassier units were the senior cavalry and generally held in highest regard. At the beginning of the Franco-Prussian War (1870–1), the Prussian army list had two guard and eight line regiments, and these were probably the best equipped, mounted and trained heavy cavalry regiments in Europe. Except for the Garde du Corps and Guard Cuirassiers, the regiments were named after their place of recruiting, following the tradition of the Napoleonic Wars: 1st Silesian, 2nd Pomeranian, 3rd East Prussian, 4th Westphalian, 5th West Prussian, 6th Brandenburg, 7th Magdeburg and 8th Rhenish. Each consisted of four squadrons of 150 men, and a 200-man depot squadron.

According to Prussian cavalry rules of 1860, the requisite height for service in the cuirassiers was at least 170 cm/5 ft 7 in for men and 157.5 cm/62 in for horses. For Guard Cuirassiers, they were 175 cm and 162 cm/5 ft 9 in and 64 in respectively. For comparison, the minimum heights of men and mount for dragoon and uhlan units were 167 cm/5 ft 6 in and 155.5 cm/61 in, and for hussars and their horses 162 cm/5 ft 4 in and 152.5 cm/60 in. For light guard horsemen, the line was set at 172 cm/5 ft 8 in for men and 156 cm/61 in for their steeds. Cuirassier and dragoon regiments were mounted on Holstein, Hanover and Magdeburg breed horses.

The height of horses is measured from the withers in centimetres/inches or hands, a hand being equal to 10.16 cm/4 in. In horses of similar proportions a difference in height of 1 cm (less than $\frac{1}{2}$ in), though seemingly negligible, could mean a difference in weight of 10–20 kg/22–44 lb. A Guard Cuirassier horse 162 cm/64 in tall could weigh up to 600 kg/330 lb while a hussar horse 152.5 cm/60 in tall would be about 450 kg/990 lb.

In the initial phase of the Battle of Mars-la-Tour, on 16 August 1870, a Prussian cavalry brigade made up of the 7th Magdeburg Cuirassiers and the 16th Uhlans executed a charge against the French infantry and artillery which became known as the *todesritt* (death ride). The French infantry threatened to attack the weak Prussian left wing near Vionville, jeopardizing further Prussian advances. As reinforcements failed to materialize, General Alvensleben ordered General von Bredow to charge with his brigade, consciously sacrificing them to halt the enemy until his own troops arrived. Von Bredow led his men into the charge spread out in a line, with the cuirassiers under Major Count von Schmetow on the left and the uhlans on the right, in all about 700 men. Under fire from cannon and machine-guns, the Prussians pierced the French defensive lines and cut down the artillery crews and the infantry around them. Carried away by their success, they attacked the French troops behind the first line, but were surprised by a division of enemy cavalry and routed. Less than half the brigade returned – 104 cuirassiers and 90 uhlans. The charge held the French back until the end of the day, and removed the danger to the Prussians' left wing.

Fearing new attacks, the French brought in another cavalry division, while the Prussians used their cavalry to secure the arrival of reinforcements. At Mars-la-Tour, 5,000 French and Prussian cuirassiers clashed in the greatest cavalry battle of the war.

PRUSSIAN CUIRASSIER
1871

89
7th US Cavalryman
1876

At the beginning of the American Civil War, the army list included the 1st and 2nd Dragoons, 1st and 2nd US Cavalry and the Mounted Riflemen, founded before the secession of the southern states, and the 1st New York 'Lincoln' Cavalry Volunteers, formed just before the start of hostilities. After the deafeat of the North at Bull Run in 1861, all six regiments of the Union army were renamed and listed as the 1st to 6th US Cavalry.

Immediately after the war, Congress adopted the Act on the Peace Establishment of the United States Army, and another four regiments of cavalry, numbered 7 to 10, were formed. In the new arrangement, each had 12 companies, marked with letters A to L, 60–70 strong. Troopers were armed with sabre, revolver and carbine, and from 1873 the standard issue revolver was the high-quality Colt Single Action .45 calibre.

The best known was the 7th US Cavalry, formed in Fort Riley, Kansas, under the command of the even better known George Armstrong Custer (1839–76). During the Civil War, Custer achieved quick promotion, starting as lieutenant and making the brevet rank of general at the age of 23. After the war, he reverted to the rank of lieutenant-colonel, but his subordinates always addressed him as general.

In 1876, Custer's regiment of 700 men, took part in three separate expeditions against the Sioux and the Cheyenne (one of 13 campaigns against the Indians by United States troops between 1865 and 1891). The 7th was sent out in advance of the main force to determine the exact location of the Indian encampment, but as it was known that several thousand Indian warriors were on the warpath, Custer had strict orders not to enter into major engagements. However, he came across one of the larger Indian camps and decided to attack, splitting the regiment so that he could advance from several sides. It is not clear exactly what happened during the attack, but Custer, the regimental staff and five companies were faced with the infinitely superior forces of Oglala Sioux, led by Chief Crazy Horse. Attempting to retreat, but cut off from the rest of the regiment, Custer decided to defend a ridge to the east of the Little Big Horn river. He and all his men were killed. The other companies of the 7th Cavalry had 52 dead and 53 injured in their retreat.

The only survivor from Custer's group was Captain Koeg's horse, Comanche. The severely wounded horse was treated by the regimental blacksmith and lived to a fine old age. He became mascot of the regiment and was never ridden again, simply taking his place of honour at the head of the unit on special ceremonial occasions.

7TH US CAVALRYMAN
1876

90
Nez Perce Indian Warrior
1877

The first Spanish explorers in America called the natives of the continent Indians, and others accepted this erroneous name. It is now generally accepted that the 'Indians' came from Asia, over the Bering Strait, about ten or eleven thousand years ago. The patterns of their settlement are not known, but towards the end of the sixteenth century there were about half a million Indians in North America, living in a large number of tribal communities. The several hundred tribes were in a state of constant war; disunited, and spread over a vast area, they could not put up effective resistance to the European colonizers.

In 1805, the first white explorers in the area of the Grande Ronde, Snake, Palouse and Salmon rivers, now the north-eastern border territory of Oregon and Idaho, came upon a tribe who called themselves *nimipu* (the people). Because of the ornaments some had in their noses they were dubbed 'Pierced Noses'. French trappers accepted this name, translating it into *nez percés*, and this in a form is their modern name – Nez Perces. Their way of life was similar to that of other American Indian tribes, but history has singled them out for particular reasons.

At the beginning of the eighteenth century the Nez Perces bought horses from the neighbouring Shoshoni. Thousands of horses were then bred on the rich grasslands surrounding the Palouse river; they were carefully selected, and in time became the breed now known as the Appaloosa pony.

The arrival of increasing numbers of white settlers, and constant conflicts with them, forced the Indians to move from the rich plains to the mountains. In 1873, the Nez Perces were consigned to the Wallowa reservation, and after minor clashes with settlers and the murder of several Indians, war broke out in 1877. In White Bird Canyon, some 60 Nez Perce Indians, led by Chief Joseph, attacked 11 settlers and 92 cavalrymen from Fort Lapwai under the command of Captain Perry. Three braves were lost, but 33 whites were killed and seven wounded. After that, the 200 warriors and 500 other members of the tribe had to retreat before the superior forces of General Howard. Chief Joseph led his men, evading army pursuit and troops from the forts, and it was only after numerous clashes and 2,700 km/1,700 miles covered in three and a half months, that Chief Joseph and the remnants of his tribe had to surrender near the Canadian border.

NEZ PERCE INDIAN WARRIOR
1877

91
British 21st Lancer
1898

A year after the end of the Napoleonic Wars, Great Britain introduced the lance as a cavalry weapon, the last of the European powers to do so. The 9th, 12th, 16th and 23rd Light Dragoon Regiments were converted into a new branch of cavalry – Lancers. The 19th Light Dragoons became Lancers in 1817, but were disbanded in 1821, when the 23rd became the 19th Lancers. The 17th Light Dragoons were given lances in 1822.

The 21st Lancers was a regiment which was founded five times. In 1759, it was formed as the Light Dragoons, known as the Royal Windsor Foresters, and disbanded in 1763. It was raised again in 1779 and disbanded in 1783, raised yet again as the Yorkshire Light Dragoons in 1794 and disbanded in 1819, except for one troop which had to guard Napoleon on St Helena until his death in 1821, when it, too, was extinguished. The regiment was formed for the fourth time in 1858 as the 3rd European Light Cavalry of Bengal, but disbanded in 1861, its men becoming part of the East India Company, where they were inaugurated for the fifth time, as the 21st Hussars. In 1897, the Hussars became Lancers, and the following year the 21st Empress of India's Lancers.

The 21st Lancers were given blue uniforms with scarlet facings, but in the subtropical climate of India, khaki uniforms were much more practical. In those, and with tropical helmets, the unit was transferred to Egypt in 1898, to become part of Lord Kitchener's forces for the expedition against the Dervishes in the Sudan. Photos of the period show officers and troopers on Arabian horses, which suggest that the regiment was transferred to Egypt without horses and given local mounts which could better support the conditions in the deserts. The regimental craftsmen certainly had a lot of work in adapting saddles and other equipment to the smaller Arabian horses.

At the decisive Battle of Omdurman (September 1898), the 21st Lancers came across 300 Dervishes retreating towards their fort. Kitchener ordered them to charge, and cut the Dervishes off. With a total strength of 320 men disposed in a line of four squadrons, they went on the attack. In the ranks was Lieutenant Winston Churchill of the 4th Hussars, also unofficial war correspondent for the *Morning Post*. The unit commander, Lieutenant-Colonel Martin, soon realized that he and his men had fallen into a trap, as between two and three thousand Dervishes rose from a hitherto invisible dry river bed and opened fire. The 21st had no choice but to fight their way through a mass of warriors renowned for their fanaticism and fearlessness. According to eyewitnesses, many of the Dervishes were trampled underfoot because they would not move out of the horses' path, waiting until the last moment before firing point-blank at the rider. With the loss of over 70 men and about 100 horses, the Lancers broke through the enemy line and gained a position to their rear. Colonel Martin ordered the men to dismount and open fire with their carbines. The Dervishes, caught in a crossfire, scattered to the shelter of nearby hillocks.

This charge brought the 21st Lancers the Khartoum battle honour.

BRITISH 21ST LANCER
1898

92
Boer Commando
1900

The Boers are descendants of Dutch colonists who moved to South Africa after the Dutch East India Company set up its outpost in the Cape in 1652. Settling was intensive towards the end of the seventeenth century, when large numbers of families arrived from Holland and Germany. Later, Hugenots expelled from France blended with the mass of Dutchmen already living there. The natives – Bushmen and Hottentots – were used by the colonists as slave labour.

Until 1795, all authority resided with the Dutch East India Company, then the colonists proclaimed self-rule, but in 1806, Great Britain captured the Cape. The Boers were not satisfied with the new regime: English was the only official language, they lost all senior positions, and the Abolition of Slavery Act of 1833 deprived them of their labour force. They migrated to the north and east, where they founded the Orange Free State, Natal and the Transvaal. However, this migration did not liberate them from British interference because all conquests by British subjects belonged to the crown. However, the Boers were determined on independence, and the outcome was the Anglo-Boer War (1899–1902).

The Boer republics had undisciplined but well-armed militia forces of about 47,000 men aged 16 to 60. After mobilization was announced, they gathered in regional centres and formed *commando* units. Each was headed by a *commandant*, and consisted of several field cornetcies of about 200 men, made up, in turn, of cornetcies of some 30 men. In practice, there were units numbering from 100 to 3,000. Officers were chosen by voting; if they did not prove able leaders, they were recalled and new ones chosen. Every militiaman contributed one or more horses, so the commandos were a sort of mounted infantry. Foreigners and natives were not admitted into the armed forces.

It was said that Boer boys were not given dinner if they missed a target with a rifle shot; these people were superb riders and marksmen. Both men and horses were accustomed to the South African climate, unlike soldiers brought from Great Britain, who underwent a painful period of adaptation.

At the beginning of the war, the Boers inflicted several serious defeats on the British – at Stormberg, Magersfontein and Colenso in 1899, and at Spion Kop in 1900. Commanded by Botha, De Wet, Smuts and Herzog, flying columns using hit-and-run guerrilla tactics destroyed British communications and forced them to erect a line of small forts to block Boer movement. Later occasional successes by the Boers did not stop the British from systematically isolating their units and destroying them one by one, thus deciding the outcome of the war.

BOER COMMANDO
1900

93
British Yeoman
1900

Recruiting, organizing and command of yeomanry units were in the hands of the country gentlemen who officered the force; the farmers and yeomen were the troopers, who all provided their own horses. The Volunteer Cavalry was formed in 1730, at the time of the Jacobite rebellions; local volunteer defence forces contributed their own horses, uniforms and arms. In 1794, when the country was threatened with invasion by France, to bolster defences Parliament proclaimed the Provisional Cavalry Act, which formalized this system. The act required that horseowners outfit one cavalryman for every ten horses they owned; those who owned fewer than ten horses were grouped, sharing in the expense proportionally to the number of horses they owned. An amendment to the act, which said that yeomanry cavalry could be substituted for provisional cavalry in the fulfilment of a county's quota, gave more incentive for the forming of yeomanry units, and military instructors helped to train these forces. According to the terms of the Peace of Amiens (1802), the yeomanry were retained, although provisional cavalry had been disbanded around 1800.

When the French invasion army began grouping again between 1803 and 1805, the yeomanry were recalled to the colours, and by the end of 1804 44,000 men had answered. Parliament annulled the restriction that yeomanry could be called up only to defend the country, claiming that the country also had to be defended on the Continent.

Until the South African War, the yeomanry's main task was to help the authorities, serving as a sort of national guard. Training was carried out over weekends, in lower-ranking units, and on local grounds. Several times a year the whole regiment would gather for joint training and review. The units were named after the county where they were raised, for example, the North Somerset Yeomanry, Sussex Yeomanry Cavalry, Yorkshire Hussars, and so on.

For the war against the Boers, the yeomanry system was again activated. Of 10,000 men available, 3,000 were sent to South Africa as the Imperial Yeomanry, a battalion equipped and organized as a unit of mounted rifles. By the end of the war, 32,000 men had passed through the yeomanry training system, and most of them were sent to the front. From 1901, the organization of yeomanry units was standardized: each regiment had four squadrons.

BRITISH YEOMAN
1900

94
Turkish Nizam Cavalryman
end of nineteenth century

Under Sultan Mahmud II (1803–39), a whole series of reforms began in the Turkish army, with the aim of making it similar in organization, training, armaments and tactics to the armies of western Europe. It was divided into the regular forces (*nizam*), the reserve (*redif*), and the last call (*mutahfiz*). The term of service in the active forces was six years, and recruits were chosen by a roll of the dice. It was the obligation of every young man of age to attend the rolling of the dice several times a year, and if he was not chosen within five years he was automatically shifted to the reserve.

From 1843, every regular cavalry regiment had six squadrons, and besides rifles and swords, the second, third, fourth and fifth of these were armed with lances. A squadron had 120 troopers; a whole regiment, with staff, numbered 736 men; 934, counting reserve and auxiliary personnel. In 1879, the number of squadrons was decreased to five per regiment, two regiments made up a brigade, three brigades a cavalry division. Cavalrymen were armed with American rapid-fire Winchester and Remington rifles, and inflicted heavy losses on the Russians with these in the 1877–8 war.

A volunteer cavalry force was created in 1885; it was called Hamidiye Süvari Alayari (Sultan Hamid's Unit). Regiments were organized according to the number of members of a tribe, and given serial numbers, from one up. They were called for training once in three years, and otherwise only in the case of need. Their men outfitted themselves and only the armaments were provided from imperial stocks. As the men of the Hamidiye cavalry came from various tribes, each of which had its own national costume, the Ottoman authorities chose three of the most common national costumes and decreed that men had to answer the call to arms dressed in one of them. The men also had to wear special tags on their clothes, with the name and number of their regiment, so that they could be distinguished from the ordinary populace.

In 1869, the Turkish cavalry consisted of 186 active squadrons and 50 volunteer regiments (20 Cherkezi, 30 Kurdish and Arab), and in case of war, large numbers of auxiliary and irregular units (*basibozuk*) were also called up. There were also auxiliary armies from Egypt, Tunisia and Tripoli under the Turkish flag. In 1876 the auxiliary contingent from Egypt was ten cavalry regiments: four of hussars, four of dragoons and two of lancers. Each had five 122-man squadrons.

The translation of basibozuk is 'broken or bad head', and a popular explanation for this term is based on the fact that in Ottoman Turkey the various races, faiths, religious orders, classes and professions were told apart primarily by their headgear. In the reforms, European-type uniforms were introduced into the army, and army and state employees had to wear the *fez*. The people were allowed to wear whatever they wanted, so they were called basibozuk, as was the irregular people's cavalry. About 10,000 basibozuk cavalry from Asia Minor, Kurdistan and Syria took part in the Crimean War, and an attempt was made to turn them into a disciplined fighting force, primarily by the English general, Bitson, but these efforts were fruitless.

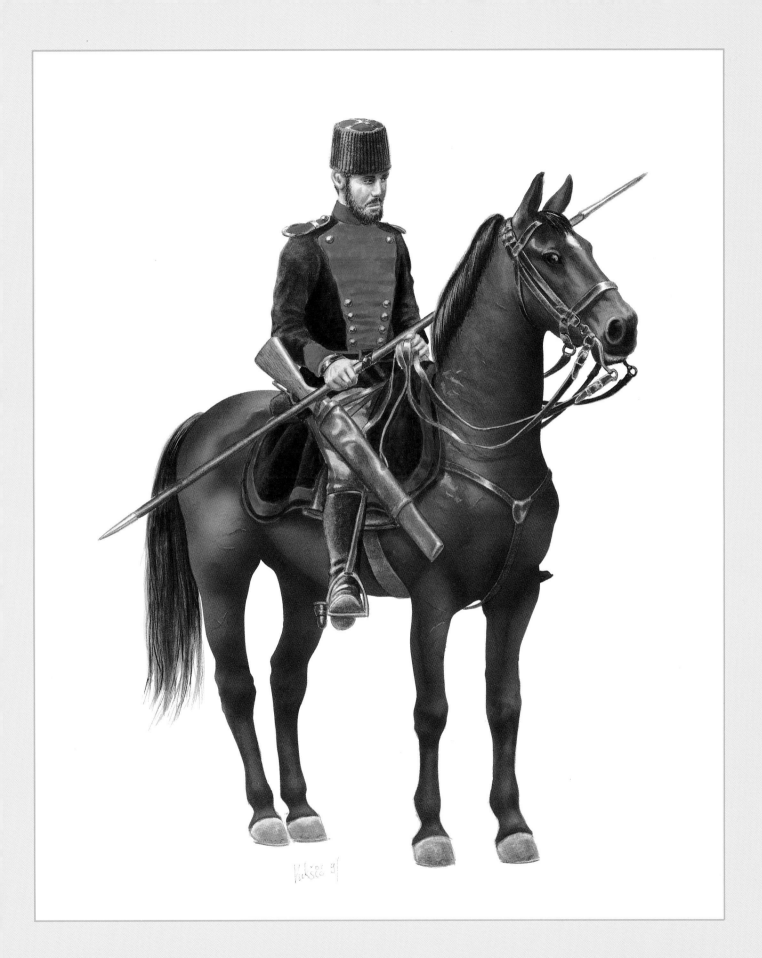

TURKISH NIZAM CAVALRYMAN
end of nineteenth century

95
Canadian Mounted Policeman
early twentieth century

In the first half of the nineteenth century, because of the Industrial Revolution in Great Britain, Canada was flooded with immigrants. This was when mass settlement in Canada really began: over 120,000 people went there in the five years between 1827 and 1832. Urban environments developed along the sea coast and the great lakes, with European-type economies. Further to the north and west, in the vast forests and mountains, the natives (Indians) and settlers hunted and traded in furs. The fur trade was controlled by several large companies, whose interest was to stop further settlement and preserve the hunting grounds.

In 1867, when the Dominion of Canada was established, the government took control of Prince Rupert's Land (named after the brother of King Charles II, best known as a cavalry commander in the English Civil War) and allowed free settlement, but the arrival of settlers in the North Saskatchewan River area caused the revolt of the *metis* (half-breeds of French settlers and Indians) and the Indians, led by Louis-David Riel. To put down this insurrection, the government dispatched an expedition which included two militia battalions raised for this purpose and, when these units arrived, the uprising collapsed virtually without bloodshed. One battalion was left to keep the peace in the rebellious area, known as Red River. A small mounted police force was detached from the battalion and stationed at Fort Garry, the administrative seat of one of the districts.

The Canadian government had to assert its sovereignty in the new territories and ensure law and order, so as to make possible the migration of settlers across the western plains. The basis was the existing police and militia forces, and the North West Mounted Police was founded in 1873. It was decided to recruit 300 men on a semi-military basis. At their first and only review, in Dufferin (now Emerson), Manitoba in 1874, the whole unit gathered in one place for the first and last time in its history, then the 318 men dispersed to their destinations. A curiosity is the march of the mounted police to the west, in which 1,650 km/1,025 miles were covered in 97 days.

The work of the mounted police included keeping law and order, reconnoitring territory, informing the central authorities of the situation, guarding public property, helping settlers, relaying information and warnings, rescue missions, and so on. Mounted patrols were the most common way of keeping in touch with the local population.

In 1920, the force was renamed the Royal Canadian Mounted Police. Today, in keeping with the spirit of the times, the 18,000 members of the service are called the Royal Canadian Mounted Police/Gendarmerie Royale du Canada (RCMP/GRC).

CANADIAN MOUNTED POLICEMAN
early twentieth century

96
US Cavalryman
c. 1912

In the second half of the nineteenth century, the most powerful nations of the period, Great Britain and France, extended their colonial empires to vast areas of Africa and Asia, as, to a lesser degree, did other European powers. Only much later did America join the process of colonial acquisition, and its first target was Cuba, then ruled by Spain. A local uprising and the mysterious explosion of the USS *Maine* in Havana harbour were pretext enough for American armed intervention. Thus began the Spanish-American War of 1898.

The US expeditionary corps consisted of two infantry divisions and one of cavalry. The cavalry had about 4,000 mounted men in five regiments, and its horsemen were armed with the modern Krag model 1896 carbine and Colt model 1894 revolver. The 1st US Volunteer Cavalry Regiment – recruited in Texas, New Mexico, Arizona and Oklahoma – was dubbed the 'Rough Riders' by the press. As coincidence has it, two future national leaders charged that year at the head of cavalry regiments: Lieutenant Winston Churchill at Omdurman, and Lieutenant-Colonel Theodore Roosevelt with the Rough Riders at San Juan Heights in Cuba. Roosevelt jumped on a horse and led his dismounted men against fierce enemy fire which disabled every fifth trooper. The future president of the United States was unhurt, the enemy was vanquished, and he became a national hero overnight.

On Cuba, with its subtropical climate and lush vegetation, the American cavalry was forced to operate mainly dismounted, like dragoons. The Americans conquered Cuba, but little remained of the Wild West aspect of their cavalry.

A similar expedition, and for similar reasons, was dispatched to the Philippines. Between 1899 and 1901 the American government sent nine cavalry regiments dressed in new khaki tropical uniforms to those islands, each regiment having about 1,200 men divided into 12 troops. They differed from ordinary infantry only in their armament. After the end of the Philippine campaign, despite its overseas experience which did not favour the mounted arm, the US formed five new cavalry regiments, numbered 11 to 15, and from 1906, a machine-gun platoon was added to every regiment. In 1912, the cavalry was given new uniforms, and protective goggles were used in the desert areas around the Mexican border.

A civil war which was to last for nearly ten years started in Mexico in 1910. American troops in the south, near the busy border with Mexico, increased their battle readiness to prevent raids by guerrilla bands. In 1916, troops commanded by General 'Black Jack' Pershing crossed into Mexico on a punitive expedition of four cavalry regiments – the 7th, 10th, 11th and 13th – infantry and artillery. Their mission was to stop border raids and capture the Mexican guerrilla commander and folk hero Pancho Villa. Villa was not caught, but the expedition put about 500 guerrillas out of action and clashed with Mexican government troops. Fearing that this incident might escalate into open war, Pershing withdrew to American territory.

US CAVALRYMAN
c. 1912

97
Bengal Lancer
1914

The development of the Indian army under British rule ran parallel with colonial expansion. The first Indian troops were organized by the British East India Company, shortly after it established its first outposts in the mid-eighteenth century. These consisted of European mercenaries and local men, whose task was to protect the trading posts. After the end of the Seven Years War in Europe, three armies were formed in India – Madras, Bombay and Bengal. Low pay, innovations which offended the religious sensibilities and ancient traditions of the natives, and especially social and economic change brought about by British rule were the causes of frequent mutinies. The largest of these, known as the Indian Mutiny (1857–8), led to the abolition of the East India Company and the introduction of dual rule. The provinces under direct rule made up British India, while 560 Indian states were ruled by local princes who were vassals of the British crown. During the mutiny, all the regular and some of the irregular Bengal regiments had been disarmed.

In 1861, the Anglo-Indian army was reorganized, and a fourth army formed in Punjab. The Bengal army was completely shaken up, and its numbers made up with loyal soldiers. Nineteen cavalry regiments, known simply as the Bengal Cavalry, were formed again, designated by the numbers 1 to 19. The 8th Bengal Cavalry had formerly been the 18th Irregular Cavalry, and 9th 1st Hodson's Horse, the 12th 2nd Sikh Irregular Cavalry, the 18th 2nd Mahratta Horse, and so on. As these units were armed with lances, their name was soon changed to Lancers.

All Indian cavalry, save four regiments of the Madras Light Cavalry, were organized according to the *silladar* system, which remained in use until the beginning of World War I. At the beginning of the nineteenth century, irregular cavalry was enlisted according to the old system of the country, where in return for a down payment the soldier would come complete with horse, arms and accoutrements, but after the reorganization of 1861 the government paid the regiments according to the number of men they had. Because of the need for uniform dress and equipment, the regimental staffs took care of these matters, as well as command functions; part of the funds was used, for example, for baggage animals. Soldiers in these units were paid more than in other regular regiments, but weapons were the only thing given directly by the government to the soldier.

The Bengal Cavalry regiments were made up of men of different races and creeds, but to avoid conflict within the regiments, squadrons were made up of members of one class, race or religion. All had the same uniform, but they were allowed to wear turbans which denoted their religious adherences. In 1897, the 2nd Bengal Lancers had one squadron each of Sikhs, Jats, Rajputs and Hindu Mahometans.

The Bengal Lancers took part in many of the British colonial campaigns, including Egypt in 1882 and Sudan in 1884–5, as well as in World War I, against the Germans on the Western Front and the Turks in the Middle East.

BENGAL LANCER
1914

98
Arab Warrior
1914

After defeat in Ethiopia in 1896, Italian imperialist tendencies sought another outlet in the Mediterranean area. The choice fell on Libya, a remote province of the Ottoman Empire, the acquisition of which would strengthen Italian positions in the Mediterranean and open a new way into the interior of Africa. In September 1911, Italy sent an expeditionary corps of 15,000 to Libya. Turkey, occupied with war in the Arabian peninsula, had no capacity to resist, but called upon the inhabitants of Libya to wage a holy war against the invaders.

The coastal areas were inhabited by hunters and shepherds of the related Berber tribes, who had been there since ancient times, and by the Arabs, who had come later. They were swift mounted warriors, who attacked from ambushes, and who had for centuries honed tactics which, in today's terms, were tantamount to guerrilla warfare in small detachments. When the war against the Italians began, the natives, with the help of Ottoman officers, were a significant fighting force, with basic units, called *adwar*, numbering between one hundred and two hundred men. Each unit had a military commander and at least one Ottoman officer as adviser. The warriors were armed mostly with old single-shot rifles, some provided by the Turks and others captured. They were dressed in their traditional garb, the *kaftan*, well suited to desert conditions. The horses they rode were of the so-called Barb breed, with a lot of Arab blood and similar characteristics: great stamina and the ability to live on very little.

With the advantage of modern weaponry, a fleet and some air support, Italy succeeded in capturing the coastal areas. However, they suffered several serious defeats, and in the middle of 1914 a supply column with large numbers of modern rifles and ammunition was captured by the Libyans. When World War I began, Turkey opted for alliance with Germany and Austria-Hungary, so Italy, Britain and France became its enemies. The Arab movement Sanussi, supported by Turkey and headed by Ottoman officer Nuri Pasha, took up arms against the British in Egypt and the French in Algeria and Morocco, while continuing the campaign against the Italians in Libya. Several thousand Arabs from the Sahara were organized into regular units, dressed in Ottoman uniforms and given batteries of cannon. In 1914, the Sanussi scored several military successes, and captured some large oases held by the British and French.

The regular colonial troops were, for the most part, transferred to the European theatre of operations, which is why the North African holdings were protected by inadequate forces. France and Britain had to recruit members of loyal local tribes and organize them into militia units, in dress and tactics very similar to their opponents. Fighting in the desert did not die down until the beginning of 1918, when the Sanussi movement fell apart.

ARAB WARRIOR
1914

99
Austro-Hungarian Dragoon Officer
1914

In 1866, Prussia forced Austria into an unfavourable peace settlement in only six weeks. On the Italian front, things were going well for Vienna, but this was small recompense for defeat by the traditional enemy. The result was extensive reorganization of the army in 1868; the effects were most apparent in the cavalry. When war with Prussia began, Austria had 12 regiments of cuirassiers, two of dragoons, 14 of hussars and 13 of uhlans. Traditionally, it was Austrians who served in the cuirassier units, Poles and Bohemians in the uhlans, Hungarians and Borderers in the hussars, and one of the dragoon regiments was Italian and the other Bohemian.

Cuirassiers were the only type of unit considered heavy cavalry, the rest as light cavalry. After the reform, the imperial Austrian and royal Hungarian armies became the Austro-Hungarian army. All cuirassier regiments were turned into dragoons, that is, all Austro-Hungarian cavalry became light. This was a radical step compared with what the Prussians, French and Russians were doing at the time. Weaponry was standardized; for example, the M.1861/69 sabre was used by dragoons, hussars and uhlans alike. Horse equipment also became standard, and only the Hungarian regiments retained some unique elements. From 1884, the lance was abandoned as an uhlan weapon.

In 1909, new pike-grey (*hechtgrau*) uniforms were introduced, but after pressure from the nobility, who served mainly in the cavalry, the emperor decided that cavalry units could retain the traditional colours. The dragoons also kept their helmet, the uhlans the *czapka* and the hussars the *shako*. The number of dragoon regiments was increased to 15, and they were allowed to keep their light blue tunics, while trousers for all units were madder red (*krapprot*). The standard greatcoat was brown and all ranks were issued with a fur-lined and trimmed *pelz*. The M.1905 helmet, modelled on the traditional helmet introduced in 1796, was covered with grey linen, and the red side cap seems to have been the preferred headgear on active duty, regardless of rank. From 1915, the standard field-grey uniforms worn by the infantry became obligatory in the cavalry too; instead of their distinctive head-dresses, they were issued with field-grey side caps.

Before the beginning of the war, Austro-Hungarian cavalry regiments were organized into divisions, each consisting of two brigades. These had two regiments each, and the regiments, in turn, six squadrons. Unlike the Western Front, where there was little cavalry activity, the Austro-Hungarian cavalry on the Galician and southern Polish fronts often clashed with Russian mounted forces, up to division strength, especially in the initial positional phase of the war. Although the front became relatively stable, cavalry was again used intensively on both sides during the Austro-Hungarian spring offensive in Galicia in 1915.

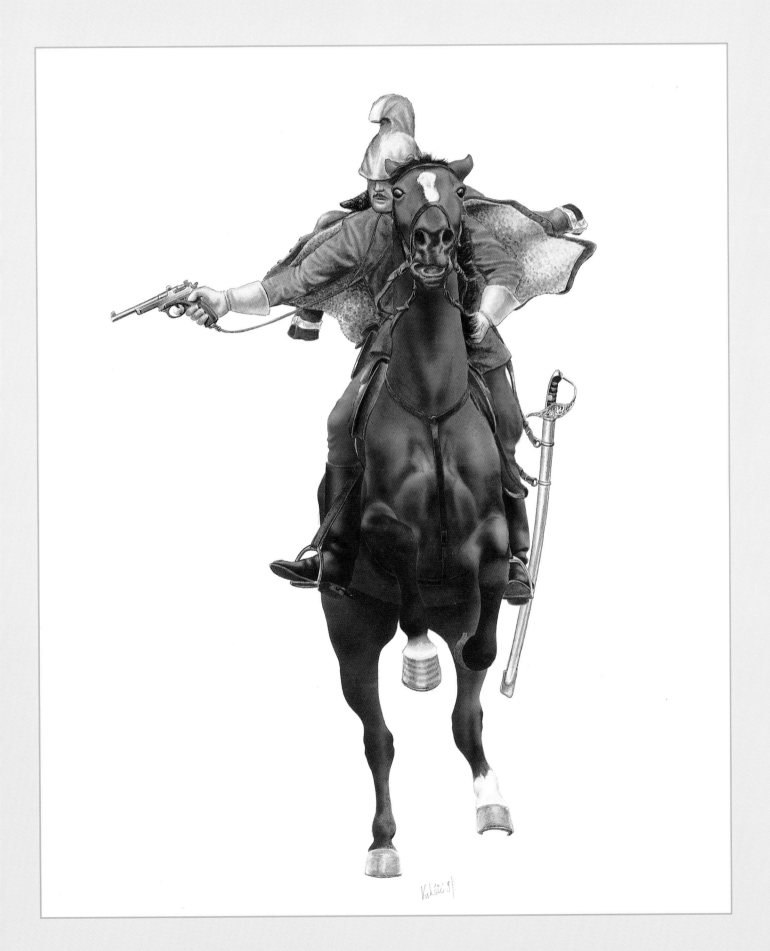

AUSTRO-HUNGARIAN DRAGOON OFFICER
1914

100
Russian
Cavalryman
1914

During the reign of Emperor Alexander III (1881–94), the Russian army abandoned the European trends in uniform fashion and chose designs closer to traditional folk costumes. In 1882, the *pickelhaube* helmet and *shako* were abolished in favour of the *shapka* head-dress, and soldiers were re-clothed in uniforms similar to the peasant garb (*rubaska*). All line cavalry regiments were changed to dragoons, so the army list counted 10 guard, 51 dragoon and 51 Cossack regiments.

Alexander III was succeeded by the last emperor, Nicholas II, who continued the habit of his predecessors and changed the army's uniform to a new cut. At the beginning of the twentieth century, soldiers were issued with white uniforms, which proved impractical and easily visible on the battlefield during the Russo-Japanese War of 1904–5. A decree of 1906 introduced an olive-green khaki colour for all uniforms. In winter, a fur cap and a long coat made of coarse grey-brown wool (*shinels*) were added. In 1907, dragoon regiments which had been hussars and uhlans reverted to their previous identities, and were also given back their parade uniforms from the mid-nineteenth century. Finally, however, this applied only to the guard.

The threat which the alliance of Austria-Hungary and Germany presented to Europe forced France closer to Russia, and France helped the modernization of the Russian army with money and up-to-date industrial technology. When war broke out in 1914, Russia, though not ready, attacked Germany and Austria-Hungary. As one military analyst wrote, initially the Russian cannon were of poor quality, the men were in the wrong places, and the most important means of troop transfer – the railways – were swamped by horses and their fodder. It was not an auspicious beginning for the largest cavalry force in the world.

In 1914, there were 122 regiments: 13 guard, 20 dragoon, 20 uhlan, 18 hussar and 51 Cossack. Guard regiments had four squadrons, those of the line six. All troopers were armed with the M.1891 carbines, calibre 7.62 mm, and the *shasha* sabre, while the first lines of uhlan and Cossack regiments also had lances. The Cossacks were divided into two groups: the Steppe (*stepnoy*), Christians, and the Caucasian (*kavkassky*), mostly Muslims.

Cavalry was organized in divisions, each of which had a regiment of dragoons, hussars, uhlans and Cossacks, and one or two batteries of horse artillery.

On the eastern Prussian front, both the Russian and the German cavalry fought mainly on foot, but the Russians conducted extensive mounted operations against Austria-Hungary.

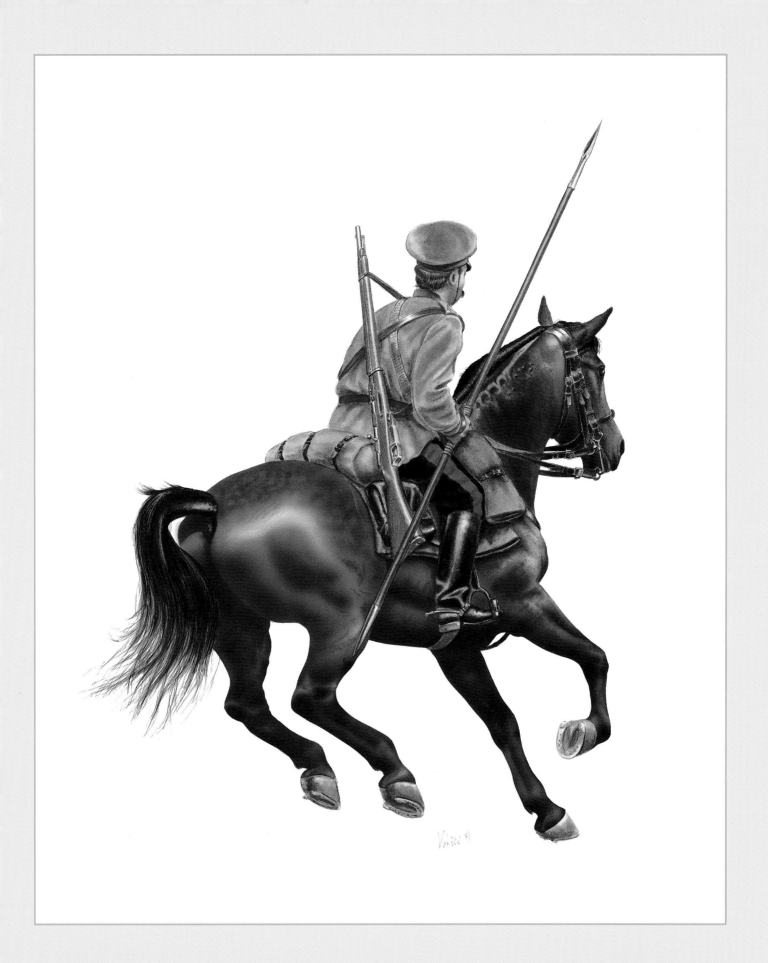

RUSSIAN CAVALRYMAN
1914

INDEX

Page numbers in italic indicate an illustration.